LIVING
AND
LEARNING
MATHEMATICS

D1560389

LIVING AND LEARNING MATHEMATICS

Stories and Strategies for Supporting Mathematical Literacy

DAVID J. WHITIN
University of South Carolina

HEIDI MILLS
University of South Carolina

TIMOTHY O'KEEFE
R. Earle Davis Elementary School
Cayce, South Carolina

Foreword by Jerome C. Harste

HEINEMANN
Portsmouth, NH

Heinemann Educational Books, Inc.
361 Hanover Street   Portsmouth, NH 03801
Offices and agents throughout the world

The publishers and the authors wish to thank the children and their
parents for permission to reproduce material in this book, and to the
following for permission to quote from previously published works:

Pages vii–viii: From Oliver Sacks, *The Man Who Mistook His Wife for a
Hat and Other Clinical Tales* (New York: Simon & Schuster, 1985), pp.
185–90. Copyright © 1970, 1981, 1983, 1984, 1985 by Oliver Sacks.
Reprinted by permission of Summit Books, a division of Simon & Schuster, Inc.

Every effort has been made to contact the copyright holders and the
children and their parents for permission to reprint borrowed material.
We regret any oversights that may have occurred and would be happy
to rectify them in future printings of this work.

Library of Congress Cataloging-in-Publication Data

Whitin, David Jackman, 1947–
    Living and learning mathematics : stories and strategies for
supporting mathematical literacy / David J. Whitin, Heidi Mills,
Timothy O'Keefe ; with a foreword by Jerome C. Harste.
        p.   cm.
    Includes bibliographical references.
    ISBN 0-435-08303-1
    1. Mathematics—Study and teaching (Elementary)   I. Mills, Heidi.
II. O'Keefe, Timothy.   III. Title.
QA135.5.W467   1990
372.7—dc20   89-39556
                                                          CIP

Cover photo by Timothy O'Keefe.
Figure 7–1 by Heidi Mills.
Other photos by David J. Whitin.
Designed by Wladislaw Finne.
Printed in the United States of America.
10 9 8 7 6 5 4 3 2 1

CONTENTS

FOREWORD

Jerome C. Harste

*When I first met the twins, John and Michael, in 1966 in a
state hospital, they were already well known. . . . The twins,
who were then twenty-six years old, had been in institutions
since the age of seven, variously diagnosed as autistic, psychotic
or severely retarded. Most of the accounts concluded that,
as idiots savants go, there was "nothing much to them"—
except for their remarkable "documentary" memories of the
tiniest visual details of their own experience, and their use of
an unconscious, calendrical algorithm that enabled them to
say at once on what day of the week a date far in the past
or future would fall. . . . [During one visit] a box of matches
on their table fell, and discharged its contents on the floor:
"111," they both cried simultaneously; and then, in a murmur,
John said "37." Michael repeated this, John said it a third
time and stopped. I counted the matches—it took me some
time—and there were 111.*

*"How could you count the matches so quickly?" I asked.
"We didn't count," they said. "We saw the 111."*

*Similar tales are told of Zacharias Dase, the number
prodigy, who would instantly call out "183" or "79" if a
pile of peas was poured out, and indicate as best he could
—he was also a dullard—that he did not count the peas,
but just "saw" their number, as a whole, in a flash.*

*"And why did you murmur '37,' and repeat it three
times?" I asked the twins. They said in unison, "37, 37,
37, 111."*

*"How did you work that out?" I said, rather hotly. They
indicated, as best they could, in poor, insufficient terms—but
perhaps there are no words to correspond to such things—
that they did not "work it out," but just "saw" it, in a flash.
John made a gesture with two outstretched fingers and his
thumb, which seemed to suggest that they had spontaneously
trisected the number, or that it "came apart" of its own
accord, into three equal parts, by a sort of spontaneous,
numerical "fission." They seemed surprised at my surprise—
as if I were somehow blind; and John's gesture conveyed an
extraordinary sense of immediate, felt reality. Is it possible, I*

said to myself, that they can somehow "see" the properties, not in a conceptual, abstract way, but as qualities, felt, sensuous, in some immediate, concrete way? And not simply isolated qualities—like "111"-ness—but qualities of relationship? (Sacks 1985, pp. 185–90)

"To think in mathematics is to think in 'relationships' and patterns of relationships," says Alt Eden, a graduate student in mathematics at Indiana University. His explanation mirrors that received by Vera John-Steiner (1985) from James D. Finley III, a famous mathematician: "I think in a different language, I think in mathematics." He elaborates:

In quantum mechanics, particles have particular properties; they change in time. So when I think of a wave-pocket, I have a picture in my mind of a pencil. Yes, a pencil and a little bell curve that gets wider and wider along the pencil, and this generates a cone. So when I am calculating, I have all kinds of pictures of cones in my head which intersect. (John-Steiner 1985, p. 184)

"I remember looking at the bathroom floor, and observing the different patterns that I could see by combining larger and smaller tiles," says Reuben Hersch, coauthor of the award-winning book *The Mathematical Experience*. "I also did arithmetic in my mind, rather obsessively, adding things endlessly, and looking for patterns in numbers" (John-Steiner 1985, pp. 174–75).

"The words or the language, as they are written or spoken, do not seem to play any role in my mechanisms of thought," wrote Albert Einstein. "The physical entities which seem to serve as elements in thought are certain signs and more or less clear images which can be voluntarily reproduced or combined" (1945, p. 142).

I decided to use this foreword to let mathematicians tell their tales as well as raise the question of what it is like to think in mathematics. Too often schools are "verbocentric" institutions, in which success is dependent on the ability to manipulate language in the abstract. Such curricula silence children whose ways of knowing are other than language. They don't serve us well either. We all lose opportunities to expand our communication potential.

Like the mathematicians quoted above, *Living and Learning Mathematics* tells a tale. It's the story of how a group of teachers create a classroom environment that gives children the opportunity to think in mathematics.

These teachers are good whole language teachers. They use what they know about learning language to improve the mathematics curriculum. If Morris Klein is right, they use a common approach to the solution of mathematical problems to solve their own problems:

Many great mathematical papers have used ideas or methods that had already appeared in the solution of other problems. Mathematicians do not always admit this, though some have. However the major point is that reading related material may be the best way to get the mind started on a new channel of thought and because the reading is related, this new thought might be the right one. (John-Steiner 1985, p. 190)

The curriculum Whitin, Mills, and O'Keefe develop invites children to use mathematics and language as tools for learning. Like good Dr. Sacks in the twins story, they value the mathematical strategies that children bring to school, and they use these as the basis for encouraging ownership. Children are invited to create stories that communicate their observations and experience mathematically. In so doing, if the mathematician John Howarth is right, they are asked not to pretend to be mathematicians but to engage mentally in the real thing:

I make abstract pictures. You reduce the number of variables, simplify and consider what you hope is the essential part of the situation you are dealing with; then you apply your analytical techniques. In making a visual picture it is possible to choose one which contains representations of only the essential elements—a simplified picture, abstracted from a number of other pictures and containing their common elements. (John-Steiner 1985, pp. 84–85)

Living and Learning Mathematics sees curriculum as a mode of inquiry for both teachers and children. Children are invited to do original research using mathematics as a tool for learning. They internalize the learning process and come to realize that, as Thomas Kuhn has explained, *discovery commences with the awareness of anomaly, i.e., with the recognition that nature has somehow violated . . . expectations. It continues with a more or less extended exploration of the area of anomaly. And it closes only when . . . the anomalous has been the expected. (1970, pp. 52–53)*

I see this book as a starting place. It's the story of how some whole language teachers saw an anomaly and took steps to resolve it. They would be the first to admit that we have far to go. Nonetheless, the stories and strategies discussed here for supporting mathematical literacy are ones upon which children and educators can build.

PREFACE

The Setting

R. Earle Davis Elementary School is located in Cayce, South Carolina, just outside of Columbia. It is a large elementary school in Lexington School District no. 2, serving approximately 670 students from diverse socioeconomic, rural, and urban neighborhoods. There are thirty-six classrooms ranging from programs for four-year-olds through grade five. The district has recently developed transition first-grade classrooms for children who have completed kindergarten but who do not appear ready to work successfully in traditional first-grade settings. The classroom that will be highlighted throughout this book is one of the two transition first-grade classrooms at Davis Elementary. Timothy O'Keefe, the classroom teacher (together with a talented Chapter One tutor, Mrs. Sandra Pees), works collaboratively with the children to create an enticing environment in which all participants work together as teachers and learners.

The Characters

The twenty children featured here were placed in Tim's classroom because of their kindergarten teacher's recommendation and because of their performance on a first-grade readiness test. While Tim recognizes the inherent problems with homogeneous groupings based on test-score data, he has come to see that the group is truly heterogeneous. Each year the transition children arrive with tremendously diverse backgrounds and abilities. He values the natural variations in his children's experiences and capitalizes on their complementary strengths when planning for the classroom.

These children have been identified as having special needs, but this label has not influenced Tim's approach. Instead of seeing them as children with deficiencies that need to be remediated, he regards them as capable learners. He attempts to understand the learning strategies and concepts that the children bring with them to the classroom; he then creates instructional invitations that build on these understandings. He accepts the children where they are as learners and takes them as far as they can go during their time together. He too adopts a learner's stance and continues to change and grow with his students.

At the conclusion of the school year, those children who are academically and socially prepared will be promoted directly to second grade. The other children, who the teacher and parents feel would benefit from a first-grade experience, will move into one of the other five first-grade classrooms at Davis Elementary.

In addition to the primary participants in this classroom, David Whitin and Heidi Mills, assistant professors in elementary education at the University of South Carolina, have worked collaboratively with Tim and the children. Together, they have assumed coteaching and research responsibilities one full day per week for the entire school year. They have attempted to devise an integrated curriculum that values mathematics and language as tools for learning. Although all three of them were involved in leading class discussions, implementing strategy lessons, videotaping classroom experiences, and gathering curriculum materials, they decided to use Tim's name throughout this book as a convenience for the reader.

The Plot

We hope the voice of the teacher as researcher comes through in this book. While our theory was not neatly in place when we began our work together, we did hold common beliefs about language learning. Our whole language philosophy of learning, which arose from our educational training at Indiana University with Jerry Harste and Carolyn Burke, was confirmed and extended through our classroom experiences. Ken and Yetta Goodman, Jerry Harste, Carolyn Burke, Virginia Woodward, Donald Graves, Frank Smith, Lucy Calkins, and others have strongly influenced our understanding of the reading and writing process. Their work has helped us develop a language arts program focused on process and also leads us to ask further questions about how we might apply these beliefs across the curriculum.

We knew that there was a connection between how children learn language and how they learn mathematics, and so we took what we knew about language and began to explore mathematics from that perspective. We began by asking questions like these:

1. How is learning mathematics like learning language?
2. What are the characteristics of learning experiences that promote mathematical literacy?
3. How can we create a balanced, integrated curriculum that encourages children to explore their own interests while providing experiences we feel are necessary to the development of mathematical literacy?

As we explored these questions we began to see the power of the work of Philip Davis and Reuben Hersch (1981), Howard Gardner (1983), and Elliot Eisner (1981). Their emphasis on alternative ways of knowing and on the nonredundant potential of each communication system helped us to reconsider the uniqueness of the mathematical system. Their ideas made sense to us given what we believed about the learning process, but it wasn't until we attempted to implement them in the classroom that we truly appreciated them. These theorists have clearly shown the value of language, art, music, and drama as ways of constructing and sharing meaning. Here we will focus on the power of learning about and through mathematics.

The Script

Language stories provide the foundation of this book. The stories come from everyday experiences in this classroom. We chose to use stories because they preserve the wholeness of events without distortion; the events are not stripped from their natural contexts.

The stories and their corresponding dialogues come from videotapes, field notes, team-meeting notes, still photographs, and literacy artifacts. The complementary nature of these data helps us preserve and study the meaning of events in context. Alternative sources of information make it possible for us to consider the process from various perspectives. For example: Two of us might be taking detailed notes during a learning experience while the other one is videotaping the interactions. When we combine the information, we are able to see a more complete picture of the event.

This book is organized around significant issues that have helped us understand how children learn mathematics and how we can develop a curriculum that is consistent with their learning process. In choosing the stories, we have focused on an exploration of patterns in learning rather than on a chronological presentation of events. Because of this organizational decision it might appear that it is the activities that we value. However, this is not the case. Our intent has been not to create a "how to" book but to describe the processes by which certain questions and beliefs about how children learn shaped our curricular decisions. For us, this book has become not an ending, but rather a beginning place from which to ask new questions and pose further hypotheses. We hope it does the same for you.

ACKNOWLEDGMENTS

There are many people who provided us with inspiration and insight during the preparation of this book. While we could never mention all of the people who touched us in this way, there are several who come to mind as being enormously helpful. Our families, friends, and colleagues encouraged us and became our sounding boards during the actual writing process.

Several people gave feedback and counsel during various drafts of the manuscript. Jerome Harste, Carolyn Burke, Evelyn Hannsen, Kathy Short, Diane Stephens, Marjorie Siegel, and Phyllis Whitin provided thought-provoking suggestions and invaluable guidance. Not only did they help us fine-tune the book, but often they would ask just the right question to help us clarify theoretical and practical issues in our own minds. Their own work has inspired us to look even further into the "why" in what we saw. Each has played an important role in our professional lives.

Dr. Richard Kemper provided for many of the practical aspects of our study, including release time and videotapes. Although his history with us was short, he believed in us and supported us from the beginning.

Sandra Pees was the tutor in our classroom. Her quiet, kind, unassuming way with children became a model for us all.

Mary Lou Fassett, Sally Hale, and Patricia Diederich were among our first mentors in the classroom. Their friendship and guidance has helped us to grow up personally and professionally. Though many years have passed, the lessons we've learned from them never will.

John Litton and Carol Martig were truly supportive administrators who always had the best interests of the children in mind. They believed in Tim as a teacher and trusted the educational decisions he made.

Zachary Mills Paquette, his parents, and his grandparents helped us envision how we might create a learning environment at school that is consistent with authentic learning experiences at home. Zachary really pushed us as "kid-watchers." He demonstrated that two-year-olds know more than we had realized.

We appreciate the many hours that Ruthanne O'Keefe spent carefully editing our manuscript. Her observations helped us consider the clarity of our text from an outside reader's perspective.

Philippa Stratton helped us get this project off the ground. Her discussion with us about mathematics in whole language classrooms helped us refine our questions and conceptualize how we should report the work we had been doing together.

Toby Gordon valued our thinking, while at the same time helped us maintain focus and remain cognizant of our audience. What else could we ask of an editor?

Donna Bouvier did a superb job of coordinating the editing and production of the manuscript. We learned a great deal in working with her.

Pat Carver and Joyce Crosby invested many hours in front of the word processor when preparing this manuscript. Their patience and tireless efforts were extremely helpful.

Finally, our heartfelt appreciation goes out to the children in our class whose inspiration was unintentional but far stronger than any other source. We are grateful for their love, friendship, trust, and learning demonstrations. They remain our greatest teachers. More than anyone else, they show us how important it is to continue to be learners.

1
SUPPORTING
MATHEMATICAL
LITERACY

**Coming to know something
is not a spectator sport.**

**Stephen Brown and Marion Walter
The Art of Problem Posing**

"What color do you like?" Jermaine inquired with a sheet of paper and box of crayons in hand. Crystal responded quickly, "I like orange." Jason echoed her reply: "I like orange too." They both watched Jermaine as he selected an orange crayon from the box and made two distinct horizontal slashes at the top of the paper. His second band of color ran into the first. He remarked to himself, "Two for orange." Crystal and Jason returned to work on their puzzle while Jermaine approached James with his personal color survey (Figure 1–1). James hesitated momentarily and then chose purple.

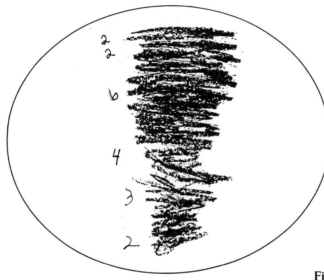

Figure
1–1
Jermaine's
color survey

Meanwhile, Katie conducted a survey of her own. She walked about the room, asking her friends, "What is your favorite animal?" As each classmate communicated a choice, Katie drew a picture of each one (Figure 1–2). Earlier in the day her teacher had read to the children an article about giraffes from a *Ranger Rick* magazine. The children were in the middle of an exciting and productive animal unit, and they were intrigued by their latest findings about giraffes. Consequently, several giraffes appeared on Katie's survey. Rashaun explained his choice for giraffes by remarking, "I like giraffes. They have to spread out their legs to get a drink of water like this." Rashaun got down on all fours, spread his arms out wide, and pretended to drink water from a pond. Katie acknowledged Rashaun's demonstration, colored an orange giraffe, and proceeded to

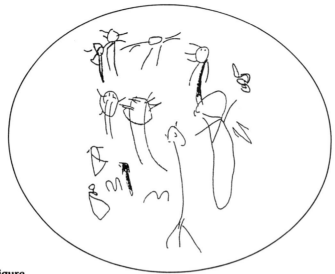

**Figure
1–2
Katie's
animal survey**

ask Mrs. Pees, the class tutor, about her favorite animal.

Jermaine found numerous children who liked red better than any other color. He had five children in a row vote for red. Next he had a few independent selections: one purple, two blue, one black, one pink, one blue, one yellow, one red, and finally one more blue. Having completed the page, Jermaine returned to his teacher to report his findings. Although several markings for the same color ran together, Jermaine had been careful to keep a mental record of the numbers behind these bands of color. He began sharing the survey's results: "Two people wanted orange. Two people were for purple." He then paused, counted to himself, and remarked, "Six people like red." He asked his teacher to write the numbers down as he tallied his markings. He continued, "Three kids liked blue plus Mr. O'Keefe so four for blue."

Katie waited for a class meeting to report her findings about the class's favorite animals. She held her paper for all the children to see, naming each animal as she counted aloud. After reporting each category, she shared the total number of votes for each animal.

The Significance of These Stories

Jermaine and Katie accepted an open-ended, instructional invitation to conduct a survey on a topic of their choice. In the process of making decisions about the content of the surveys and various ways to collect, organize, and display their information both children expanded their understanding of mathematics. Although their surveys might look unconventional from an adult perspective, the processes used to construct them reveal logical, systematic, and rule-governed thinking. Katie's survey resembled a traditional pictograph. It nicely conveyed her classmates' choices. Jermaine's use of color was appropriate for the question that he was posing. They each chose a form of graphic representation that seemed to fit best the kind of information they were seeking. These decisions allowed the children to pursue an in-depth exploration about the nature of mathematics as a communication system. Their undertaking showed that the sign system has unique forms and structures that can be adapted to the question at hand. They discovered that color and pictures used in conjunction with other graphic decisions can clarify the documentation of choices.

While they were learning about the communication potential of surveys they were simultaneously exploring content and procedural knowledge. In responding to Katie's survey, the children revealed their knowledge of animals. Like many of the children, Rashaun discussed the attributes of his choice—giraffes—and, in addition, dramatically demonstrated how giraffes eat and move. Sign systems such as language, mathematics, drama, and art do not operate in isolation; instead, children naturally use various communication systems to construct and share meaning.

Procedural options were also clear as the children made choices about the best ways they could represent the information they were collecting. They could see that mathematics was much more than a rigid set of rules, skills, or drills. They found it to be a useful tool for exploring their world and sharing their discoveries with others.

Jermaine and Katie were both children who were placed in a transition classroom because they were identified as not being "ready" for first grade. Yet they and their classmates display sophisticated reasoning when engaging in authentic mathematical experiences. We believe that it is encumbent upon schools to provide educational experiences like these that enhance, and not restrict, learning.

Mathematical Literacy

M. A. K. Halliday (1975) states that any literacy engagement has the potential for people to learn language, learn about language, and learn through language. This model of literacy learning can be a lens through which we view not only written and oral language but mathematics as well. In fact, we can consider any communication system—whether it be mime, sculpture, or music—as the center for this perspective on learning. As children engage in mathematical experiences there is the potential for them to learn mathematics, learn about mathematics, and learn through mathematics. Although all three aspects are inherent in all literacy engagements, children often intentionally highlight one of them for special attention (Rowe 1986). Let us look more closely at these three dimensions of literacy and view their implications for mathematics learning.

LEARNING MATHEMATICS

Mathematics, like language development, is essentially a process of construction, not acquisition. Learning mathematics involves learning how to use mathematics in one's social world to meet one's particular purposes and intentions. The focus of attention should always be on the meaning that is being communicated rather than on the form of the mathematics itself. Children gain insights into the global purposes of mathematics by measuring dinosaurs, counting teeth, and raising fish. Mathematics is never apart from living. The unfortunate obsession with drill, computation, and rote learning masks the real purposes of mathematics. Children can best learn mathematics by being exposed to its multitudinous uses. Mathematics is for recipes to be doubled, plants to be measured, fruit to be divided, prices to be compared, polls to be interpreted, time to be estimated, meals to be ordered, bills to be paid, and marbles to be shared. Mathematics is not an act but an event, an experience. Its purposes are not divorced from the lives of children but emanate from the intentions of the children themselves. Katie and Jermaine were learning mathematics as they explored some of its uses. They were coming to view mathematics as a vehicle for gathering and tabulating answers to meaningful questions that were relevant to them. As they shared their findings with their classmates, they were also teaching each other about important mathematical concepts.

Learning mathematics is also a collaborative venture. Children do not learn mathematics apart from their social world. Rather, the global purposes of mathematics are embedded in the problems that learners encounter, the plans they formulate, and the decisions they make. Effective mathematics instruction provides children opportunities to pursue their own interests. The teacher then becomes not only a facilitator and resource but also an active participant in these investigations.

LEARNING ABOUT MATHEMATICS

Learning about mathematics involves learning how mathematics functions as a system in particular contexts. Children explore the "how" question—"How does this system of mathematics work?"—by noting such things as "Hey, these two triangles make a square." They might wrestle with certain formatting decisions, such as "Do I write three red chips and three blue chips as 3 3 6 or as 6 3 3?" Children may also have to decide how to coordinate art, written language, and mathematics to communicate their story. As children focus on the system of mathematics itself they sometimes note certain mathematical principles, such as "I see that 4 and 2 is like 2 and 4; I just turned them around." They may also uncover some mathematical relationships. Daehoon, for instance, held up three fingers on one hand and one finger on the other hand. He then turned one finger down on his first hand and raised another finger on his right hand and remarked, "Look, 3 and 1 is just like 2 and 2. They both make 4." He continued to raise and lower fingers on each hand to demonstrate his discovery. On other occasions children may focus their attention on the outward appearance of their numerical observations. Jermaine categorized a set of fourteen animals and then recorded them in various ways: $14 + 0$, $13 + 1$, $12 + 2$, $11 + 3$, $10 + 4$, and so on. He looked at his mathematical names for 14, and then turned to the teacher and commented, "You know, 14 and 0 doesn't look like as much as 8 and 6 because it has a 0. But it is. It's got 14 and that's a lot." All of these examples show how the children naturally pursued some of their own discoveries as they explored the system of mathematics itself. Because of their active role in these investigations, the children perceived themselves as mathematicians in their own right.

LEARNING THROUGH MATHEMATICS

Learning through mathematics involves using mathematics to explore and expand one's world. During their study of dinosaurs the six- and seven-year-olds in this class were constantly comparing and contrasting various dinosaurs. The illustrations they viewed in books and the imaginative stories they told convinced the children that some of the largest dinosaurs could have stretched across the entire length of the playground. At one point during this study the children researched the lengths of the most popular dinosaurs and then transferred these measurements to the playground. They were amazed to find that even the longest dinosaur only reached to the end of the classroom building. In this way they were learning about dinosaurs through mathematics.

Aaron learned through mathematics during his study of plant life. After the children had conducted numerous plant experiments, Tim read them *The Carrot Seed* by Ruth Krauss. The children were then invited to create their own plant stories. This experience allowed Aaron to demonstrate much of his current knowledge about plants. When he was asked to describe his equation of $10 - 8 = 2$, he said, "It had ten seeds. Eight didn't grow. There was two plants left. They growed" (Figure 1–3).

**Figure
1–3**

Aaron's equation $10 - 8 = 2$

**"Plants can grow in the sun.
The plants cannot grow in the dark.
Plants can grow in the rain.
Plants cannot grow in the snow."**

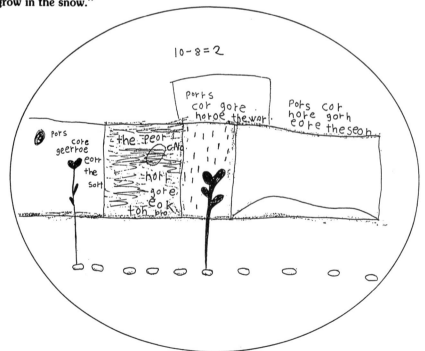

In his story Aaron also included specific reasons for the seeds' inactivity or growth. On the left-hand side of the page he colored in a yellow square and wrote, "Plants can grow in the sun." Aaron was reminded of how well all the plants did that were positioned near the classroom window. In his next square he wrote, "The plants cannot grow in the dark." He had set up an experiment of trying to grow a plant behind one of the classroom cupboards and knew the results of such an attempt. The next square demonstrates another important variable for plant growth as Aaron writes, "Plants can grow in the rain." The class had purposely not watered several plants and Aaron incorporated the result in his story. Finally Aaron included one other reason for lack of plant growth by writing above the remaining seeds, "Plants cannot grow in the snow." Thus, the only two plants that did grow, $10 - 8 = 2$, were ones that received sun and rain. Darkness and snowfall caused the demise of the others. Aaron's story serves to illustrate how he can learn through mathematics by sharing his knowledge of plants.

Learning through mathematics can also involve opportunities for children to gain procedural knowledge. Such was the case for Lena. She was conducting a personal survey of her classmates, asking each one, "Do you like to play with toys or ride your bike?" As the children responded she wrote their names on her recording sheet. After she had interviewed about eight people Tim inquired, "What have you found out so far, Lena?" She looked at her list of names but was a bit hesitant to respond because she was unable to recollect how each person voted.

"Can you think of a way to keep track of what people said?" Tim asked. Lena shrugged her shoulders and then turned to her friend Veronica for some advice.

"You could draw a picture of some toys," her friend suggested.

"I don't know how to draw toys," Lena replied. The two girls discussed the matter further and finally decided to draw a circle next to the name of each person who chose bikes. Lena read each name again from her list, reinterviewed each person to confirm his or her preference, and recorded a circle next to each name if it was appropriate to do so (Figure 1–4). This experience helped Lena refine her procedural knowledge of personal surveys. As she attempted to reconstruct the choices

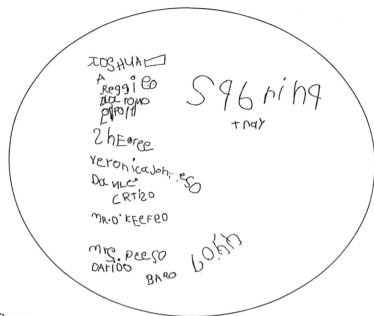

**Figure
1–4
Lena's
personal survey**

that had been made she realized that the information she had gathered was insufficient. Her strategy of drawing circles helped her to distinguish between the two options. In this way Lena was learning through mathematics that certain recording systems convey more information than others and that it was important to differentiate, in some way, among choices.

Toward a Model of Mathematical Literacy

The perspective on language learning proposed by Halliday is also a helpful model for viewing mathematical literacy (Figure 1–5). After all, mathematics is a language too. It is a communication system that we use to explore and expand our knowledge of the world. Children grow in mathematical literacy when they have regular opportunities to investigate the purposes, processes, and content of the mathematical system. All three aspects are inherent in a single mathematical experience. The children, as constructors of their own knowledge, decide which aspect to draw out for special attention. Their decisions reflect their individual interests and previous experiences as well as their current intentions and interactions with those around them. In addition, teachers sometimes create experiences that highlight one of these aspects so that the children will attend to it as part of a natural context. For example, children learn about the various purposes of mathematics as they measure dinosaur lengths on the playground, interpret results of a personal survey, or calculate the most economical plan for a field trip.

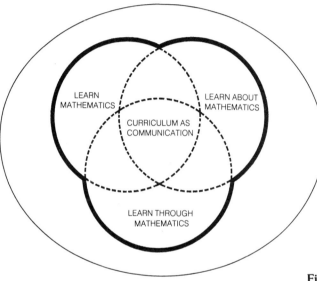

Figure 1–5 Model of mathematical literacy

Learning about mathematics involves learners in exploring the mathematical system itself. Children are encouraged to experiment with how the system works, such as devising their own recording system to convey their numerical observations. If children are given the freedom to explore how the mathematics system operates in different contexts and are encouraged to share their findings, they feel trusted as learners and feel encouraged to take risks and devise unique solutions. This support gives children increasing responsibility for their own learning. In written language development, the form of the message develops through use; this is also true in mathematics. Mathematical literacy is defined not as a mere familiarity with numerical symbols but rather as an understanding of the ideas and processes that the symbols represent. It is this notion that is at the heart of learning about mathematics.

Learning through mathematics implies that children use mathematics in all subject areas. Mathematics is an integral part of social studies as children construct maps of their neighborhood; it is a useful tool in science investigations as learners keep a daily tally of the number of eggs laid by the class turtle; and it is a natural part of the cooking area when the bakers must figure out how to divide the cookies equally. Mathematical literacy develops in response to personal and social needs. Thus, meaningful mathematical endeavors often grow from the interests and experiences of the children themselves.

Characteristics of Learning Experiences that Promote Mathematical Literacy

As teachers view mathematical literacy from Halliday's perspective they attempt to help children understand its forms and purposes. Through our work with children we have identified certain characteristics of learning experiences that promote growth in mathematical literacy.

First, *authentic mathematical experiences are open-ended; they invite children to solve a given problem in a variety of ways.* An open-ended activity requires no pre-entry qualifications before children can engage in it and demands no criterion level before they can exit. Teachers who provide open-ended learning experiences assume all children are ready to learn and are capable of using their own unique background and experiences to construct meaning for themselves.

One example of an open-ended experience occurred in Tim's transition first-grade classroom. Children had begun losing some of their primary teeth and started to share their teeth stories with each other. Tim capitalized on this interest by inviting children to record their teeth stories on a piece of paper. The children's responses were many and varied. Some stories demonstrated subtraction: "My cousin had ten teeth. He lost two teeth. Now he has eight teeth." Other stories showed more detail: "He had eight teeth. He was climbing a tree and he knocked four teeth out. He had four teeth left." Chris demonstrated a knowledge of zero when he wrote "7 7 0" and then wrote: "He had seven teeth. He was riding his bike. He fell off his bike and lost all seven teeth." Several other children told stories that required more than one operation. B. J. wrote "6 1 5 1" and then told her story: "My sister had six teeth. She lost one. She had five, but one grew back" (Figure 1–6).

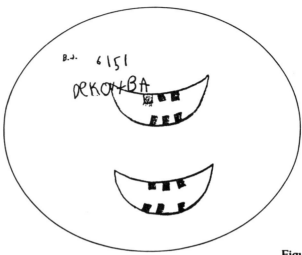

Figure
1–6
B. J.: "6 1 5 1"

In her upper drawing she crossed one tooth out to show it was gone but in her bottom drawing she reinstated the new tooth! Tim used this experience to evaluate his students' knowledge. In B. J.'s case he noted, "She seems to be investigating the relationship between addition and subtraction. I will observe and talk to her during other math activities to see if she pursues this insight and indeed has a firm understanding of this relationship." Tim also noted that even though B. J.'s written representation of her story was not conventional, lacking the necessary operational signs, nevertheless B. J. knew exactly what her marks meant and could read her story problem quite readily. A meaning-centered approach to mathematics is the cornerstone of mathematical literacy. In this classroom there was a definite shift from computational performance to mathematical understanding. It is not what children can do on the isolated pages of arithmetic workbooks that demonstrates mathematical literacy but how well they can make sense of mathematics as they engage in purposeful activities.

Second, *authentic mathematical experiences can be adapted and changed by children.* On another day in this classroom the children were discussing the different customs of various cultures at Christmastime. They discussed how people used lights and learned about the different customs of gift giving. As an extension of this unit the children were invited to write their own gift-giving stories using six presents. The children ingeniously devised their own natural extensions to this problem.

Matt recorded various combinations of six and then decided to draw and write about the contents of some of these gifts (Figure 1–7).

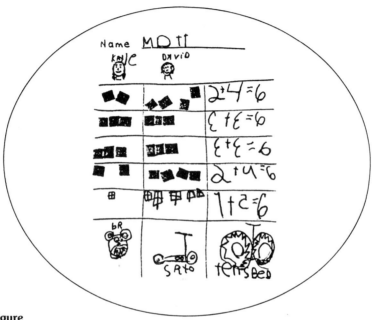

**Figure
1–7
Matt's writing about
six presents:
BR (bear),
SRTO (scooter),
and TENSBED (ten speed)**

Several other children revised this activity by giving only the same number of presents to the two people in their story. Once they realized that 3 + 3 was the only way to divide 6 evenly, they abandoned the restriction of using just six gifts and created other double combinations: 1 + 1 = 2, 2 + 2 = 4, 4 + 4 = 8, and so on. Their reasoning was "It wouldn't be fair for one kid to have more than the other!" Raphael glued down three gifts under each person several times and then wrote "3 6 3 6." When he was asked to tell his story he touched each numeral 3, and then each set of three presents and replied, "This 3," pointing to the first 3, "and the other 3 is 6." Then, placing his finger on the second numeral 3, he continued his story by saying, "And this 3 and the other 3 is 6." Thus, he created his own unique way to demonstrate the communativity principle of addition. His written observation was not recorded in the conventional manner, but it held meaning for him; that was the crucial point. It is also important to note that this child had the opportunity to talk about his discovery. As-

sessment of children's understanding of concepts is often revealed through talking and listening to them. Merely collecting
and checking off the finished product in the class record book
would have circumvented the understanding that Raphael was
able to demonstrate. When children have the opportunity to
explain what they mean, teachers gain fresh insights into how
children learn.

Third, *authentic mathematical experiences are multimodal;
they encourage children to draw on a variety of communication
systems—art, writing, reading, mathematics—to convey their
observations.* Jermaine was studying dinosaurs. Tim invited the
children to create their own dinosaur stories, and Jermaine
wrote "It was a terrible and nasty fight. The king's team won.
Brachiosaurus got beat up" (Figure 1–8). When asked to tell
about his numbers he said, "Three was here [the top three].
Then five was here. Then that made eight." Jermaine used
the same color crayon for the top three dinosaurs to indicate
that they were on the same team. This color helped to highlight
the "threeness" of this group. He also drew spots of red on
their backs to show that they were wounded. Thus, Jermaine
drew upon his knowledge of dinosaurs and integrated that
learning through art, writing, mathematics, and language.

**Figure
1–8**
Jermaine: "It was a terrible
and nasty fight.
The king's team won.
Brachiosaurus got beat up."

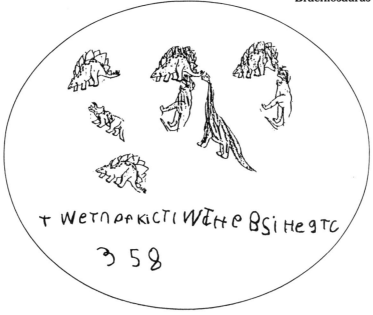

Mathematics was a natural way to convey part of this prehistoric story. Experiences such as these helped Jermaine see that numbers do not operate in a vacuum but gain meaning as they work in conjunction with other communication systems.

Graphing is another vehicle for encouraging children to use various communication systems in order to share their discoveries. Also, since there is no single best way to graph all information, children need to be given opportunites to collect and display information in their own way; they are robbed of fruitful learning possibilities if the experience is continually structured for them. Look at the example of six-year-old Curtis. The class had been studying animals and he was especially interested in camels. He had written an entry in the class newspaper about camels, and his spelling strategy for camel (KML) was shared by the teacher at their class meeting. Shortly after this sharing session Curtis decided to conduct his own personal survey. He canvassed his classmates by posing the question, "Do you like camels?" His results are shown in Figure 1–9.

**Figure
1–9
Curtis's survey:
"Do you
like camels?"**

What an ingenious way to represent his findings! He decided to write camel (KML) for those friends who said they liked camels and to record their name if they claimed they did not like camels. Curtis devised his own unique recording system to differentiate between the two responses. Thus, he was learning how he could use written language to organize the numerical data he was collecting.

Fourth, *authentic mathematical experiences promote risk taking*. Chris was trying to find different ways to share six presents between two people. After he discovered 2 + 4, 4 + 2, and 3 + 3, he began to change the total number of presents, hoping this modification would give him a different combination for six. He mumbled to himself as he changed the original set, "Now, I'm going to try 3 + 4" and "Now, I'm going to try 1 + 4." After much trial and error, Chris realized that these kind of changes gave him two different addends, which was the result he was trying to obtain, but unfortunately the sum was no longer equal to six. However, his strategy certainly made good sense. Combinations such as 2 + 4 and 3 + 3 were names for six, so why not try other pairs in hopes of uncovering other possibilities. It seemed that the appearance of the addends merely needed to be changed, such as 3 + 4 and 1 + 4, in order to obtain a different name for six. However, he later realized the result of these changes and returned to the original sum of six to find other combinations, such as 5 + 1 and 1 + 5. Open-ended tasks such as this one, which challenge children to find as many answers as they can, also encourage children to take risks and venture guesses. Because Chris took the risk of changing the problem slightly he was growing in his mathematical understanding: that is, changing the appearance of the addends may or may not affect the sum. Just as in language learning, children grow in mathematical literacy when they are willing to take some risks, stepping outside the sphere of what they know by testing out a new hunch or a current hypothesis about how numbers work. Good teachers support such risk-taking ventures; they encourage children to change some of the variables in a given problem to create a multitude of related problems. Fostering such inquisitiveness has been described as the art of problem posing (Brown and Walter 1983); it encourages the flexible use of skills and strategies by challenging children to use what they know under slightly different conditions. Schools must continue to nurture the development of such flexible thinking.

Finally, *authentic mathematical experiences encourage social interaction*. A group of transition first-grade students had been studying animals. They became interested in the eggs of certain animals when they noticed their classroom turtle, Angela, laying eggs in the sand. This observation led them to ask questions about other egg-laying creatures. Soon eggs became a temporary focus for the animal unit. One morning Tim constructed a graph at the front of the room; he wrote the three choices of fried, scrambled, and boiled eggs and drew a picture of each. As the children came over to cast their vote Tray asked, "How many can you sign up for?" The children were learning together about the rules for this particular graph. It was Tray who immediately assumed ownership of this graph. He was responsible for leading each of his classmates to this chart of choices. Before each person cast his or her vote he gave them his sales pitch for his favorite, scrambled eggs. "Now these here," he said, pointing to the boiled eggs, "you have to peel all the shell off. Yuck! And it takes so much time. And this one here," he continued, referring disdainfully to the fried egg, "is all spread out. But this one here," he said, his face breaking into a genuine smile, "is real good. You know this one. Your mama makes them. She chops them up and puts butter on them. They are good!" Thus, it was through social interaction that the children not only learned about the distinct choices but also gained information about the advantages and disadvantages of each selection.

At the class meeting Tim showed the graph and asked, "What did we find out?" Again they supported each other's growth by sharing personal interpretations.

"They all have five," observed Veronica. The children counted to be sure she was correct.

"This one looks bigger," said Sheree, pointing to the column for scrambled eggs.

"Why is that?" asked Tim.

" 'Cause there are a lot of big names there," she replied.

"And this one looks little," said Quinton, referring to the column for boiled eggs, where all the signatures were written in smaller letters. The rest of the class looked at the graph to confirm these observations and saw indeed that there was a distinct size difference in the signatures under each column.

"Did more people vote for scrambled eggs than boiled eggs?" Tim inquired.

"No, it just looks big," replied Sheree.

It was through social interactions such as these that the children were developing a healthy skepticism toward pictorial representations. Sometimes graphs can be misleading, and the deceptive use of size is a strategy that is frequently employed. Thus, the children were learning from each other as they shared observations and insights about the visual display of quantitative information.

Looking Ahead

The specific stories used throughout this book highlight the characteristics of experiences that foster mathematical literacy and demonstrate the kind of strategies that children adopt quite naturally as they create meaning for the stories they wish to communicate. The three facets of literacy engagements described by Halliday will be the lens through which these stories will be discussed and interpreted. The stories highlight the rich potential inherent in open-ended, functional experiences that invite children to explore the purposes, processes, and content of the mathematics system.

The experiences described here are not to be seen as disconnected activities that were arbitrarily presented to the class. Instead, the children played an active role in generating such topics as dinosaurs, fish, teeth, and books. In this sense, the planning was done with the children, not merely for the children. To understand the mathematical significance of these stories one must be aware of the total context in which mathematics played a part. After all, mathematics is never apart from anything else. Rather, it is embedded in what people like, in what they do, in what they want to learn. By describing the salient, contextual features of these mathematical stories, it is our hope that the reader might come to know and appreciate the children, their teacher, and the curricular decisions they fashioned together, as they simultaneously lived and learned mathematics.

2
INVESTIGATING DINOSAURS: MATHEMATICS AS A TOOL FOR LEARNING

Children will enjoy mathematics
because it will have
relevance for them
in the lives
they are living.

Edith Biggs and Robert McClean
Freedom to Learn

Just as language is not about letters, so mathematics is not really about numbers. Numbers are signs that represent quantitative ideas and relationships. When used in thoughtful, systematic combinations numbers gain usefulness just as letters do in texts. Just as we have learned that it is counterproductive to focus instruction on the form, rather than the function, of language, we have also found that children learn and remember mathematical concepts more easily when they are embedded in meaningful contexts. Mathematical literacy develops just as naturally as oral and written language. Harste, Woodward, and Burke (1984) argue that children learn about the underlying rules or structure of language as a fringe benefit of using language. It is common to see very young children reading environmental print and writing their own messages before they have "conventional control." It is important to appreciate early language utterances and reading and writing efforts as communicative events and to look for meaning in the experiences. So too in mathematics. Children gain important insights into how the mathematical system works as they learn about dinosaurs, animals, and other topics of mutual interest. In this chapter we will share many ways that Tim and the children used mathematics as a tool for learning about dinosaurs. Mathematics provided them a perspective through which they could pose their own questions and seek their own answers. Accordingly, children in this classroom rarely used numbers without tying them to stories, real problems, or investigations.

We chose to focus on Jermaine to illustrate one child's strategic use of mathematics throughout this unit of study. As we describe his learning experiences, we are able to highlight his flexible use of mathematics to learn and to teach others about dinosaurs. We have also included other children's responses to demonstrate the diversity inherent in this type of learning environment.

Before embarking on this study of dinosaurs we asked ourselves several questions:

1. How can mathematics be used as a tool for learning about dinosaurs?
2. How will children incorporate their knowledge of dinosaurs into mathematical contexts?
3. What questions will mathematics enable the children to pose?
4. How can teachers plan with children and not simply for children when devising a unit on dinosaurs?

5. How can teachers plan to teach specific mathematical concepts without isolating them from the unit of study?

We knew that mathematics would provide children with a unique perspective on dinosaur life, but we were not sure how children would use it to share and construct their findings about prehistoric life. The children helped us better understand the role of mathematics as this unit on dinosaurs progressed.

Using Mathematics to Make Curricular Decisions

The children had just completed a successful animal unit that had been initiated by Tim. Now he decided to give the children a voice in determining the next unit of study. He listed on the chalkboard several topics he was interested in pursuing. His list included outer space, plants, weather, and the human body. He then invited the children to add subjects that intrigued them.

Chris suggested sharks, which elicited an enthusiastic murmur from his classmates. However, when Rashaun suggested dinosaurs by growling it out in a dinosaurlike voice, his energy for this topic proved to be contagious. Once the list was complete, the children were given the opportunity to vote through secret ballot. Tally marks were placed on the chalkboard to record the final vote.

Allowing the children to vote on the next unit of study gave them ownership of this aspect of the curriculum. They could see their voice through the tally marks on the chalkboard. The natural use of numbers in this selection process demonstrated their functionality.

Children Use Mathematics as a Sign System to Explore Dinosaurs

After deciding to study dinosaurs, the children nearly depleted the school library's dinosaur collection. Although Tim was pleased about the children's enthusiasm, he was somewhat apprehensive because he knew very little about dinosaurs himself. He figured that the best way to begin would be to gather information from the children about what they already knew about dinosaurs and what they wanted to find out.

During a class meeting Tim admitted to the children that he

had some knowledge of dinosaurs but that he also had lots of questions and he planned on learning with them. He asked them to generate some facts about these ancient creatures as well as to pose some questions of their own. While this might seem like a reading and writing experience, several of the children, as well as the teacher, naturally incorporated mathematics into their responses. They used mathematics in combination with the other sign systems of written language and art to share their understanding.

Jermaine remembered reading about tyrannosaurus rex's extremely large, sharp teeth. Before writing what he knew about dinosaurs he referred to his book so he could accurately portray their size. He wrote, "Dinosaurs have six-inch teeth." Next, he illustrated tyrannosaurus rex and carefully drew the teeth to scale. Then he took a ruler from the mathematics area and meticulously drew a six-inch tooth beside his scaled drawing (Figure 2–1). He turned his paper over and recorded the ques-

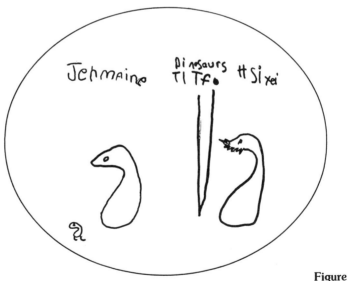

Figure
2–1
Jermaine: "Dinosaurs have
six-inch teeth."

tion he was interested in pursuing: "Is dinosaurs still alive?" (Figure 2–2). Later we discussed the fact that some creatures, such as alligators and crocodiles, have remained relatively unchanged for thousands of years, but that dinosaurs did become extinct.

Ernie also used mathematics in conjunction with art and

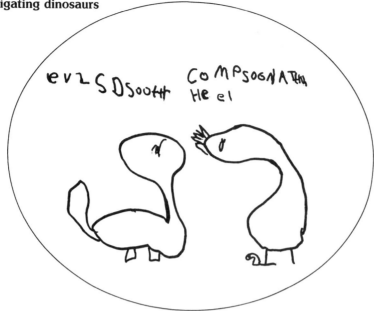

Figure
2–2
Jermaine: "Is dinosaurs
still alive?"

language when sharing what he knew about dinosaurs. He drew a large four-legged dinosaur complete with eggs cracking in a nest. Then he wrote, "The dinosaurs lived long before the Pilgrims" (Figure 2–3). Ernie strategically tied together two events that occurred long ago and placed them in a chronological order. In a sense, Ernie tied two "long agos" together to create a single time line of one "very long time ago." Here again the unique potential of the mathematics system for draw-

Figure
2–3
Ernie: "The dinosaurs
lived long
before the Pilgrims."

ing comparisons enabled Ernie to link his past knowledge of Thanksgiving to his current interest in dinosaurs.

Ernie's question, "Why did they die?" (Figure 2–4), was also asked by some of the other children. It is an astute question that is still debated by scientists today.

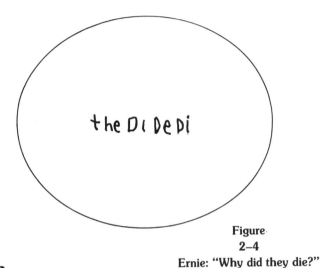

Figure 2–4
Ernie: "Why did they die?"

Looking at Literature from a Mathematical Perspective

After Tim read *Danny and the Dinosaur* (Hoff 1958) to the class, he invited the children to draw and write a response to the story. Once again, Jermaine investigated an interesting mathematical concept. At first, Tim was perplexed by Jermaine's written work (Figure 2–5). After Jermaine read "He changed back and forth into a different dinosaur," Tim asked him to explain. Jermaine picked up a copy of the book and opened it to a page that showed the dinosaur much larger than houses and buildings. Jermaine then flipped to another page that depicted the dinosaur barely larger than a lamppost. He went on to show other discrepancies in the drawings. "See, he was on two legs." Then he turned to another page. "Now he was on four legs. He is trying to trick us!"

Tim was impressed with how perceptive Jermaine was at noticing the inconsistencies in the illustrations. He admitted to Jermaine that he had read the story several times without noticing this change in perspective. Jermaine beamed with pride. The fact that Jermaine attended to these differences in spatial relationships shows us that he went beyond the basic content

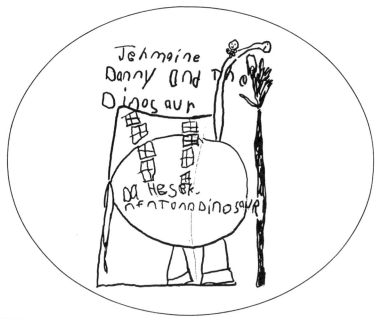

**Figure
2–5**
Jermaine: "He changed back
and forth
into a different dinosaur."

of the story in order to think about the illustrations mathematically. Jermaine understood the importance of an accurate and consistent portrayal of the characters. He perceived the relative size of the dinosaur to be a "trick" of the illustrator, and he was unwilling to be deceived.

His observation that the dinosaur switched from two legs to

**Figure
2–6**
Jermaine's journal:
"Dinosaurs
are bigger
than a house."

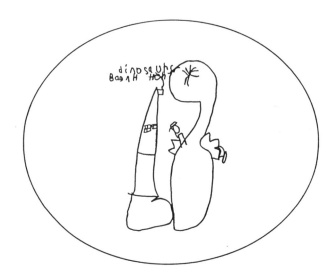

four was significant because Jermaine knew that, with a few exceptions, those that walked on two legs were predators who fed on other dinosaurs and those that walked on four legs were generally the more peaceful herbivores. Jermaine's observation highlighted the fact that the number of legs that dinosaurs stood on were signs that conveyed important information about these extinct reptiles.

We found that Jermaine further explored this notion about perspective while writing in his personal journal (Figure 2–6). Thus, Jermaine continued to think about dinosaurs and their spatial relationships as he recorded additional comparisons on his own initiative.

Invitations that Highlight Mathematics

In the midst of the dinosaur unit, Tim invited the children to use pictures of dinosaurs to create their own number stories. The open-ended instructions were simply to use dinosaur pictures, crayons, markers, pencils, scissors, glue, and construction paper to create original number stories. As the children constructed their individual stories, they were able to express some of their content knowledge of dinosaurs while exploring various aspects of the mathematical system, such as classifying, sequencing, patterning, using different formats for addition and subtraction (vertical and horizontal), and counting by twos. As they worked together the children asked questions, provided assistance, and commented on each other's discoveries. What they learned from each other went far beyond what they could have done individually.

Jermaine seriously contemplated the placement of his dinosaurs as he created the scene for his story. As he carefully colored each picture, he used language to direct the action in his drama. "Then brachiosaurus, he got beat up by this stegosaurus," he whispered under his breath as he glued brachiosaurus into place. Jermaine used bright red splotches to indicate his wounded victims. The drama continued to unfold as he meticulously added each new character.

Talking partly to the others at his table and partly to himself, Jermaine told his story complete with gestures. "See, these four here," Jermaine remarked as he pointed to a group of stegosauruses, "were against these four. And then they started to fight. Brachiosaurus got beat up. And then they wanted a rematch and he cheated." Jermaine pointed to triceratops, indicating the cheater. "He ran and dig his horns into him. And he took him, and he took him, and he took him." Jermaine pointed to the corresponding pairs of battling dinosaurs and concluded grandly, "And the king's team won!"

After creating a mathematical story through drama and art, Jermaine quite naturally expressed his thoughts in one succinct line of print. "It was a terrible and nasty fight. The king's team won. Brachiosaurus got beat up" (Figure 2–7). Jermaine used

**Figure
2–7**
**Jermaine: "It was a terrible
and nasty fight.
The king's team won.
Brachiosaurus got beat up."**

numbers throughout his oral text by describing two groups of four for the opposing teams and by pairing each team in a one-to-one fashion to carry out the action. He also used numbers to indicate the position of the dinosaurs on the paper. Although his marks are not conventional, Jermaine's equation does represent how the dinosaurs were grouped on the paper. As he explained, "Three was here, then five was here, then that made eight."

At the same time, Daehoon illustrated basic addition and subtraction vignettes on both sides of the same paper. Those sitting near Daehoon benefited by the ease with which he showed these two operations. Using the fingers on one hand, Daehoon calculated his addition problem before putting pen to paper (Figure 2–8). Then, Daehoon cleverly used black X's to show the deceased dinosaurs and clarified his picture story with an equation (Figure 2–9).

tar was
3 2 cam
tar was 5

$3 + 2 = 5$

$3 - 2 = 1$ tar was
3 and 2 was
did tar was 1

**Figure
2–8
Daehoon's illustration
of 3 + 2 = 5:
"There was three.
Two came.
There was five."**

**Figure
2–9
Daehoon's illustration
of 3 − 2 = 1:
"There was three,
and two died.
There was one."**

Rashaun approached this activity with enthusiasm; his love for telling stories and his passion for dinosaurs were wonderfully woven together in his tale. He began by drawing a tall thin tree on the left side of the paper and then glued three brachiosauruses next to it, eating peacefully. While the plant eaters were grazing, Rashaun placed three attacking tyrannosaurus rexes behind them. Then the blood began to flow! Blood began dripping from the mouths of the kings while he made red gashes in the sides of the herbivores. Knowing that Rashaun would create an exciting piece, other children looked on as he used a linear series of letters, letterlike marks, and numerals to document his ideas (Figure 2–10). The final product does not come

**Figure
2–10**
Rashaun: "There were
six dinosaurs.
One dinosaur was eating
off the tree.
The king ate him
and left his bones.
He ate some more.
Three were left."

close to reflecting the excitement that was generated by Rashaun's dramatic reading of his story. Rashaun added a number of details that were not necessary to the number story but were indeed relevant to his interpretation of dinosaur history. It has been recommended that children be exposed to mathematical problems that contain extraneous information so that they must sift through the data to determine what is necessary to solve the problem. Rashaun shows us that children naturally include supporting details, which are not important to solve the mathematical portion of the problem, but are necessary for creating interesting and realistic narratives.

Creating Dinosaur Games

One morning several children accepted Tim's invitation to create their own board games based on their knowledge of dinosaurs. The children enjoyed playing board games during their "free choice" time. These games provided an interesting way to learn addition and subtraction facts, as well as a context for learning how to follow rules and cooperate with peers. Tim viewed this experience as another opportunity for the children to share their knowledge about dinosaurs through a new and different medium. He wondered how they would represent mathematical ideas in this new context.

Matt began by drawing a winding green path across the top and down the right side of his large sheet of tagboard. While marking off tiny squares, he counted the number of spaces his players would need to move in order to reach their destination. Next, he drew a huge version of tyrannosaurus rex in the center of the board. As he was designating the beginning and end of the game by writing "start" and "finish" in his invented spelling, Sharmarla glanced over and exclaimed, "Oooh, that is neat!" Matt barely acknowledged her compliment as he continued to work intently (Figure 2–11). Matt entitled his game "KA D

**Figure
2–11
Matt at work
on his dinosaur game**

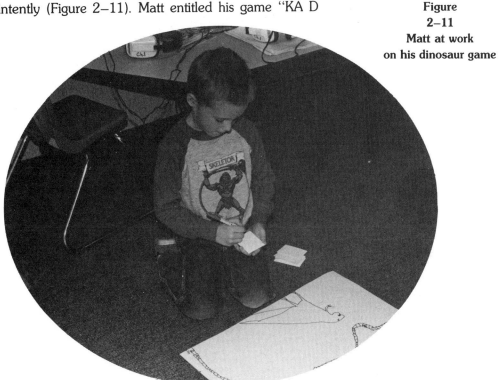

DNS GE" (Catch the Dinosaur Game) and then spent the next fifteen minutes making direction cards for his potential players. Each card had a number with an arrow pointing up or down. When asked to read it, Matt replied, "That means go eleven ways back." He continued to share other cards and read, "Fourteen frontwards, ten back. . . ." One of the earliest known symbols for subtraction was an arrow that indicated some kind of movement backward and forward. Matt's game board was much like a curved number line along which the players used arrows and numerals to change their position.

Raymond also worked independently, although he was positioned close enough to Ernie and Chris to borrow some of their good ideas. Raymond's game board was filled with specific directions for the players to follow. "If somebody go down this way," Raymond said as he pointed to a specific square on his board, "NO means go back two spaces." He continued to explain the rules to his colleagues by pointing to illustrations and their corresponding texts. Referring to a picture of a vicious dog with the word "dog" written conventionally Raymond said, "That's the dog bite right there. If they go on that one, they have to go back up seven spaces. That's the ocean right there; ocean means go back seven. If they go up this way a brick wall is there, they have to go back twelve. This supposed to be quick sand. This supposed to be the stop," as he pointed to a space with a bright red stop sign. "This supposed to be the ghost haunted house. This supposed to be the hot old sun" (Figure 2–12).

**Figure
2–12
Raymond's dinosaur game**

Figure
2–13
Chris and Ernie's
"nice and good"
dinosaur game

Like Matt, Raymond used numbers and arrows to indicate the progression through the maze of obstacles. While Matt created cards to guide the players, Raymond used dice as well as his own set of board game symbols. Raymond clearly tied ideas in his own game to others that he had played in the past by including danger and obstacles to impede the player's progress. Finally, Raymond selected four different plastic dinosaurs as game pieces.

Meanwhile, Chris and Ernie worked collaboratively. Chris started by drawing a snakelike path across the tagboard. Carefully, he and Ernie divided it into squares of different sizes and colors.

"Be careful, Chris," cautioned Ernie. "Make it nice and good." Chris made a large blue circular shape in the lower left quadrant of the game board and proceeded to fill it in.

"What's that for?" Ernie inquired.

"I'm making an ocean. If somebody gets in the water, they got to wait down here."

"When do they get out?" asked Ernie.

"Only when it's their turn again," answered Chris.

Then Ernie extended the blue of Chris's ocean to the lower right corner and reached for a brown marker. Ernie drew a rickety bridge over the water. When asked about the bridge Ernie stated matter-of-factly, "It has holes in it and when brachiosaurus walks on it he would break the bridge and fall down and his long neck would stick out of the water" (Figure 2–13).

Ernie and Chris seemed to incorporate more content knowledge about dinosaurs than either Matt or Raymond. Perhaps this was because the collaborative nature of their venture enabled them to share and build on each other's understanding of these creatures. The children had recently discussed the idea that brachiosaurus, being one of the largest dinosaurs, probably escaped from its enemies by retreating into deep water. There it could wait out its hungry foes and still breathe easily. Chris and Ernie used this information in their project. Their moveable pieces were more than simple markers; indeed they became characters in a drama as Chris and Ernie created different rules and restrictions for each one. For instance, the brachiosaurus would break through the bridge and have to skip a turn, but the triceratops, who operated under different restrictions related to its size and general characteristics, did not have to abide by this rule. Thus, the numerical penalties assigned to each dinosaur reflected the children's current knowledge of each reptile. To play this game successfully, the children would have to count, add numbers on cubes, understand the meaning of zero when it required them to skip a turn, read picture clues, and learn more about dinosaurs like brachiosaurus. They were learning about the mathematical concepts that underpin board games while they continued to expand and refine their understanding of dinosaurs.

Measuring Dinosaurs

The children constantly referred to a poster showing a time line and the relative size of various dinosaurs compared to animals of today. When noting this interest, Tim saw a need to follow the children's interest and graphically display the various sizes of these great creatures. Together, he and the children used several means to determine the length and height of seven of the more popular dinosaurs. Included in the list were plateosaurus, stegosaurus, trachodon, allosaurus, brontosaurus, brachiosaurus, and diplodocus.

One group marked off dinosaur lengths in the hallway, while another group went outdoors to see if any dinosaurs were long enough to reach from the school building to the tennis courts. This second group used tongue depressors, paper flags, and markers to create flags with the names and drawings of each dinosaur. Armed with these materials, as well as rulers, yardsticks, and a list of dinosaur lengths, Tim and the children ventured outdoors to mark off these lengths on the playground. The class gathered at the wall under the classroom window to predict how far away they thought they would need to post their respective markers. "If a plateosaurus was standing here, where do you think the tip of its tail would be?" Tim asked. A couple of children estimated the length by taking twenty steps. Next, the children and Tim used the rulers end-to-end to measure the distance. The pennant was tapped into the ground at the twenty-foot mark. Since plateosaurus and stegosaurus were both twenty feet long, two markers were placed side by side.

The children figured out a shortcut for determining the length of the other dinosaurs. They realized that they could find trachodon's length of thirty feet by merely marking off another ten feet. Likewise, they stepped off another five feet to reach the length of allosaurus.

Once the lengths of all seven dinosaurs had been ascertained, the children returned to the wall as their starting point.

"Look out and see the flags," said Tim. "Those are the lengths of our dinosaurs. Let's take a walk and visit each one." The group marched together until they reached the first pennants.

"Let's look back to the wall," said Tim. "From there to here stretched the plateosaurus and stegosaurus."

"But there were longer ones," said Rashaun.

"That's right," Tim replied, as the group looked ahead to the rest of the flags. "Let's march on." Each time the group paused to look back, and then ahead, to gain a better understanding of the relative size of these creatures. Prior to this measuring experience many of the children had imagined that some of these dinosaurs could stretch all the way to the tennis courts. Now, as they stood at the last flag, which represented the longest dinosaur, the ninety-foot diplodocus, the children realized that even this giant reached only halfway to those tennis courts. As the children moved from one flag to the next they were coming to know mathematics as a system for highlighting comparisons and for placing objects in a rank order so that we can better understand their relationships. The children were learning about this potential of the mathematical system as they explored a topic that was interesting to them (Figure 2–14).

Figure
2–14
Jesse predicts the length
of stegosaurus

Dinosaur Graphs

Graphs and surveys were among the most popular activities during free-choice time. Children learned mathematics as well as specific content knowledge as they used them both during their study of dinosaurs. From Halliday's perspective, they were learning about graphs as well as through graphs. The following description of a dinosaur graph created by the children illustrates this point. (Graphs and surveys were such an integral part of this curriculum that we have devoted a complete chapter to these strategies. Although only one example will be cited here, graphs and surveys proved to be an important vehicle throughout this theme unit for discovering and sharing knowledge about dinosaurs. See O'Keefe, in press.)

After being introduced to graphs at the beginning of the year, the children recognized their value in organizing and interpreting information. Graphs had been used for a variety of purposes, including finding out about class preferences (Which book do you like best? Which color is your favorite? Which version of Pinocchio do you prefer?); making class decisions (What should we have for the Friday party? What should we name the turtle? What color should we paint the puppet theater?); and learning more about our world (Do you like to handle worms? Which one do you think runs the fastest, a horse or a rabbit?).

Which Dinosaur Do You Like?

One job children were often invited to do before the morning meeting was to participate in a graph or survey. On this particular morning Tim asked Raymond to help him devise a question about dinosaurs and then wrote out his response, "Which dinosaur do you like?"

As others saw the creation, they also wanted to be involved. April wanted to draw tyrannosaurus (the king), Jesse offered to draw stegosaurus, Ernie volunteered for brontosaurus, and Raymond requested triceratops. Graphs were posted early in the morning so each person could have a chance to participate. Raymond stationed himself close to the graph to answer any questions or explain what the children needed to do (Figure 2–15).

**Figure
2–15
"Which dinosaur
do you like?"**

Sharing Results

The last order of business before quiet writing time each day was to share what the class observed about the morning's graph. The discussion often began with an open-ended question.

"What do you notice about the graph, Raphael?"

"Most people like the king" was his immediate reply.

"Anyone else?" Tim asked.

"Four people voted for stegosaurus and two people voted for triceratops," added Crystal.

"That's six!" Ricky chimed in.

"How do you know?" Tim asked, challenging Ricky to extend his answer.

"I just know, two and four is six, that's all."

Next Tim asked a few children to explain why they made certain choices. This question allowed them to share information they had learned about specific dinosaurs.

"Why did you vote for the king, Raphael?"

" 'Cause I like him. He eats a lot."

"Jesse, how about you? Why did you choose stegosaurus?"

" 'Cause he gots a big bump on the back of his tail."

"Why do you think its tail is like that?" asked Tim.

Jesse answered, "It looks like a big bat with spikes."

"He has it to protect hisself from the meat eaters," Jermaine added.

The children were learning that graphs are an important vehicle for collecting and sharing information. Since the discussion was open-ended, the children could offer their individual interpretations. They used the language of mathematics to describe results that were meaningful for them. The children had the opportunity to teach and learn from each other.

Summary

The children in this classroom capitalized on mathematics as a tool for broadening their knowledge about dinosaurs. They used mathematics to tabulate the class preferences for certain dinosaurs as well as to describe the different ways to classify certain sets of dinosaurs. Mathematics provided them a perspective for posing questions they wanted to have answered about dinosaur life. The children integrated mathematics into the rules and regulations of their dinosaur board games. They also capitalized on the potential of the mathematics system to make measurement comparisons by marking off the lengths of dinosaurs on the playground. Their interest lay in dinosaurs, but mathematics provided them unique avenues for viewing and exploring these creatures of long ago.

Personal Reflection

Several experiences surprised us during this study of dinosaur life. First, we were continually amazed at how observant the children were about the size and other important characteristics of dinosaurs. They became critical reviewers of each others' drawings as well as of the illustrations in several books. This attention to detail enabled them to classify dinosaurs in many ways. We wondered whether their opportunity to choose this unit of study contributed to this fascination for detail or whether certain science topics inherently encourage this kind of focus. The second event that surprised us was the children's interest in time lines. Before the unit began we thought the children would have little understanding of such a tool. We supposed that time lines depicting spans of millions of years would make little sense to children who were still unfamiliar with the months of the year. However, Ernie's comparison of dinosaurs and the Pilgrims demonstrated for us again that learning is a process of connecting patterns and building upon what we know. Ernie was creating his own time line based on the historical events he knew most about. We were becoming convinced that any mathematical tool, including time lines, ought to be made available to children to use.

Although we were beginning to understand better how children could use mathematics to ask certain questions about dinosaur life, we wanted to learn more about its role in other areas of study. Thus, the questions we posed for ourselves at the onset of this investigation were not the same ones we were asking at its conclusion. Now we wondered:

1. How can mathematics be used as a tool for exploring other topics in science?
2. How can specific mathematical tools, such as charts and time lines, be used in other disciplines, and how can we explore these uses with children?
3. What are other ways children can use board games to construct and share meaning?

The children were helping us see the potential of mathematics as a tool for inquiry.

3
RESPONDING TO CHILDREN'S INTERESTS

**It is wise to let the child
be one's guide in opening
the doors to learning.**

**Edith Biggs and Robert McClean
Freedom to Learn**

One way to create a functional mathematics curriculum for children is to capitalize on their interests. Whether their interests lie in baseball cards, marbles, horses, or dolls, they can be a vehicle for extending learning and inspiring mathematical investigations. By incorporating children's interests into the mathematics curriculum we provide a context in which mathematics is used in an authentic way; these interests connect mathematics to the world of children, emphasizing the functional nature of mathematics; they build on the experience and knowledge that the children have already acquired and enhance children's self-concept by valuing a topic that they already know something about.

Although we agreed on the importance of using children's interests to extend learning we were not quite sure how to begin. We asked ourselves two questions:

1. How can we best discover children's interests?
2. How can we structure experiences that invite children to use mathematics to share and explore their interests?

We did not want to impose the use of mathematics on children but wanted its use to arise naturally from the stories and observations the children wished to communicate. We still wondered whether children would use mathematics as naturally and confidently as they could use written and oral language. The children helped us answer these questions, as the following two experiences will demonstrate.

One of the topics—losing and growing teeth—occurred because Tim took the time to listen to the children as they recounted their unique dental stories throughout the year. Another topic—the birth and death of fish—originated because Tim capitalized on the daily events of the classroom to extend learning. Both of these experiences show the importance of planning *with* children, not just *for* children, to develop a functional curriculum that is responsive to their interests.

The Mathematics of Losing and Growing Teeth

Six-year-old Crystal bounded up to Tim, pointing to a wiggly front tooth (Figure 3–1): "Hey, Mr. O'Keefe, pull this one out for me. It's really ripe!"

Tim took hold of the loose tooth as the rest of the class

**Figure
3–1
"Hey, Mr. O'Keefe, pull this
one out for me.
It's really ripe!"**

gathered around to watch. With a slight twist of his fingers the tooth came out easily. Crystal was right—it was very ripe! After she had washed out her mouth and folded her tooth into a paper towel for its safe journey home, Crystal began feeling her other teeth.

"Hey, Mr. O'Keefe, pull this one out. It's loose too!" she said.

Surprised at Crystal's unbounded faith in his dental prowess, Tim felt the second tooth.

"No, it's not yet ready to come out. It's loose, but it needs some more time" was his prognosis.

As Crystal sat down, wiggling that stubborn tooth a bit more, other children began to share their own personal teeth stories.

"I'm missing four teeth," said Daehoon, opening his mouth and pointing to two large gaps. "I have two more loose teeth. Then I'll have six teeth gone."

Other children shared the details of accidents and other circumstances that surrounded the loss of their teeth. Some children were eager to point out the gaps in their mouths as visible proof of the stories they were telling. There were still others who felt it was important to show the new teeth they had recently acquired. Even though the specifics varied from child to child, everyone had a story to tell. As the children recounted their stories Tim realized that these experiences provided a natural context for mathematics. Children were describing the processes of addition and subtraction as they related their particular stories. Following the children's current interest, Tim gave the children a paper that had the outline of two mouths. The children were invited to cut out some paper teeth and tell their own teeth stories. Their work demonstrated some interesting insights into various mathematical concepts.

The stories that the children created were replete with the language of mathematics.

- Daehoon: I have thirty-nine teeth. Four fell out. I have thirty-five left.
- Crystal: I had all. Except one day I had two gone.
- Ernie: He lost three teeth. He had three more.
- Jesse: She crashed on a bike. She only has one.

The children naturally used mathematical language to communicate their stories. They were provided the opportunity to use such language to broaden and deepen their understanding of the concepts of addition and subtraction.

As the children wrote numbers to tell their stories, some embedded the numbers within the written text while others wrote them in a separate space on the paper. Although many of their mathematical equations did not look conventional from an adult perspective, all of the markings that the children created conveyed a meaningful, organized text. Joyce wrote two stories (Figure 3–2, A and B).

Figure
3–2
Joyce's two stories.
A: "9 1 8. Once upon a time one tooth fell out and then one almost grew back."
B: "8 1 7. Shamarla had one missing. And then she had seven left."

A

B

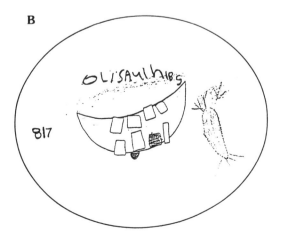

April wrote the story in Figure 3–3. She chose not to record the number of teeth her sister, Sherel, possessed before the accident. Instead she used numbers to convey those parts of the story that were of most interest to her: the number of teeth lost and the number of teeth that remained.

**Figure
3–3**
April's story: "Once upon a
time my sister named
Sherel. She had two teeth
knocked out. She had
eleven left."

In both examples the children wrote the numerals from left to right, the same direction as written language. Throughout the year the children wrote numerals horizontally—

$$2 + 3 = 5$$

and vertically—

$$\begin{array}{r} 2 \\ +3 \\ \hline 5 \end{array}$$

to tell their stories. From our observations we have found that children do not need a textbook to teach them these two different formats for writing equations. Instead, if given ownership of the process, they learn about the mathematics system by experimenting with both forms of mathematical notation on their own initiative. Neither April nor Joyce used minus or equal signs in their stories; nevertheless, their intent was clear. The important point to recognize here is that their numerical marks were intentional; they carried a story, even though they were not conventional. A major obstacle in understanding written language growth has been the confusion between intentionality and conventionality (Harste, Woodward, and Burke 1984). This same problem plagues mathematical literacy as well. There has been an unfortunate rush to make children's written equations look conventional without providing them sufficient time to refine their understanding of the mathematical concepts involved or to work out their own ways of organizing numbers to communicate their stories. It has been wrongly assumed that unless the markings are conventional, they are not intentional. But if we look at their numerals from a functional perspective—that is, to see if the learners used them to mean, to communicate, to share observations of the world—then we see the learners' efforts from a broader and more literacy-focused perspective. We see them learning about mathematics while using mathematics to learn.

In using mathematics intentionally these children not only expected their marks to be meaningful and purposeful, but they also sought to make their numerals work in concert with language and art. Both April and Joyce used art by blackening one or several teeth to show which teeth were missing. It was this drawing that supported the meaning of their written marks. Most of the children used this strategy of darkening one or more of the teeth to show which ones were lost. However, some chose to represent this action in another way. Jesse used the format of the two mouths to tell one story (Figure 3–4).

**Figure
3–4**
Jesse's story: "She crashed
on a bike. She only
has one. 3 − + 1 4."

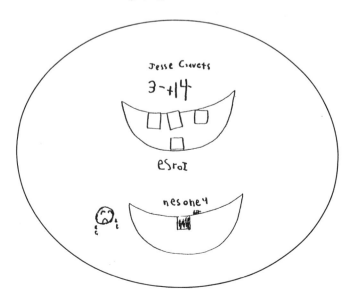

By using both pictures Jesse could convey a "before" and "after" representation. Each drawing represented a distinct point in time, while the drawings of April and Joyce combined both points of time into a single representation. Children grow and learn through mathematics when they are given control of the process and are encouraged to use various sign systems together to communicate the actions of their stories.

The drawings of Jesse, April, and Joyce also enabled them to see the inverse relationship between addition and subtraction. For instance, in Joyce's first example, 9 1 8, she can see simultaneously the original set of 9 and the resulting set of 8. In this way she could see that not only does $9 - 1 = 8$ but also that $8 + 1 = 9$. Jesse could see this same relationship by viewing the top drawing as the original set (4) and the bottom drawing as the resulting set (1). Thus, the inverse relationship of $4 - 3 = 1$ and $1 + 3 = 4$ was shown quite clearly. Piaget noted that young children have difficulty reversing the operations of addition and subtraction. However, children grow in their understanding of this relationship through authentic experiences that are connected to their interests and world.

As mathematics textbooks for young children attempt to "simplify" and pare down story problems, it is interesting to note how complex many of the problems were that the children created themselves. Raphael's work is a good example (Figure 3–5). His story and artwork convey many actions. First, the dentist pulled one tooth and left thirteen. Then, the two teeth in the lower front were also pulled and two other teeth grew

**Figure
3–5
Raphael: "The dentist
pulled one. Then there was
thirteen. And these
two pull out and these two grow
back. This one is big
and this one is little."**

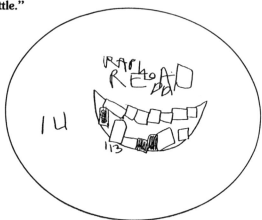

back in their place. This was a true story, and Raphael wanted to be sure that all the details were accurate. As he told his story to his classmates, he pointed to his two new teeth, making certain that they noticed that one tooth was bigger than the other. Textbooks would not have included a problem such as this for several reasons: the numbers were too large (Raphael needed to master basic facts to ten before using numbers any higher); there were too many actions (the various events described by Raphael would be too confusing for young children; it is best to limit problems to a single action); and the problem contained too much extraneous information (the size of the teeth, for instance, was merely a distracting and unimportant detail). However, Raphael defied all of these perceived constraints because he was allowed to use mathematics in an authentic way to tell his own personal story. Children surprise us with the complexity of their thinking when they are trusted as learners and given the opportunity to think for themselves. Raphael used large numbers, incorporated several actions, and included the size of his new teeth because these were significant details for his story. To see these details as irrelevant is to view his story from an adult, egocentric perspective. Instead, the information that Raphael provided was an integral part of his story, and he was careful to include all these details each time he told his story.

Mathematics in the Fish Bowl

There had been problems with the fish from the very beginning. Tim had bought two black moors, three goldfish, and one Siamese fighting fish, known as the beta, and had placed them in the class fish bowl. The beta was the only fish with teeth, and he began snapping off part of a black moor's tail. Even though he was eventually separated from the rest of the group, several of the fish began to die. The children took the first fish outside to bury it. They dug a shallow hole, which they covered with flowers, and Jesse twisted some sticks into the shape of a cross. As the children finished the burial, they stood around the hole in silence until Katie remarked, "Well, isn't anybody going to say anything?"

The children looked at Katie, and then at each other, unsure of what to say. Katie took command of the situation and said in a solemn voice, "He was a good fish."

During the next several weeks Tim brought some minnows to school. Although some of these died as well, there were several that proved to be quite hearty. It was at this time that April decided to draw her own fish story. She created it one morning, after viewing the recent condition of the classroom fish, and posted her drawing above the fish bowl (Figure 3–6).

**Figure
3–6
April reads her fish story**

She drew a picture of the mommy, with wonderfully distinctive eyelashes, and the daddy fish, along with their seven babies. She wrote her own initials, as well as those of her friends, to represent each baby fish. At first she drew only six babies, but she revised her drawing later, although she did not add another set of initials (Figure 3–7). She tallied the total number of babies as seven and then indicated that three of that set were boys. Her decision to include baby fish in her story was not a surprise to any of her classmates. Throughout the year April found ways to incorporate this theme of babies into other areas of study; during the units on animals and then dinosaurs April did considerable reading, writing, and questioning about younger animals. Her decision here to draw some baby fish serves to emphasize again April's ability to integrate her own personal interests into the larger class theme of fish.

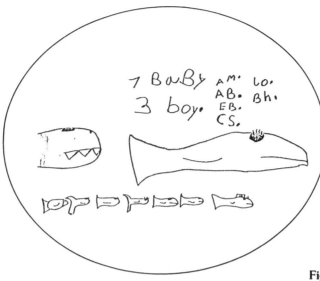

**Figure
3–7
April's drawing:
"7 baby.
3 boy."**

April's fish story prompted Tim to invite other children to create their own stories. He drew the outline of one, two, and four fish bowls on separate pieces of paper and encouraged the children to choose their own format to tell their particular story. Their responses reflected considerable knowledge about fish as well as some intriguing insights into mathematical literacy (Figure 3–8).

Since raising fish in the classroom had been such a debacle, most of the children wrote stories that contained dead or dying

**Figure
3–8
April creates another
fish story**

fish. In order to represent visually this take-away situation for subtraction the children had to devise a way to show which fish were dying. The open-ended nature of this problem allowed the children to learn through mathematics; numbers became a tool for learning that reflected the children's current knowledge of fish and past strategies in other mathematical contexts to construct their meaning. They were also learning about the purposes of mathematics as a vehicle for communicating a real classroom event. Some children, such as Chris, marked an X across the dying fish, utilizing a strategy that he had employed before (Figure 3–9). Joyce represented the dying

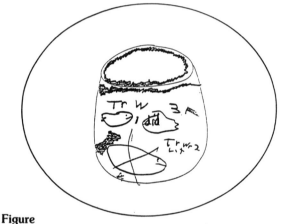

**Figure
3–9**
Chris: "There were three fish.
One died.
There were two left."

fish by giving it a different color—brown—and separating it from the rest of the group by placing it at the bottom of the tank (Figure 3–10). Her decision to use color as a distinguishing feature was also adopted by other children. As Shamarla worked on her story she verbalized her intentions: "These are the two babies, and this is the mommy, and this is the big brother, and this is the daddy. The daddy is going to die, so I'm going to color it brown, and I'm going to put it in a box." Her talking was a vehicle for planning the story she was intending to write. Her choice of the color brown matched the greyish-brown color of the dead fish that the children had found in the classroom tank. By using art as a communication system, Shamarla was able to share additional, personal knowledge of the event. Art infused her mathematical story with a richer and deeper meaning. Shamarla's efforts helped us begin to realize that textbook story problems lack this richness because they are unconnected

Figure
3–10
Joyce: "There was one
fish dead.
3 − 1 = 2."

to the lives and interests of children; instead, they tend to be stark and shallow, devoid of significant details that are a natural part of the stories that children can create themselves if they are provided the opportunity to do so.

Other children devised different ways of representing the dying fish. Matt and April each incorporated bubbles to indicate the number of fish that were still alive (Figure 3–11). The one fish that was sick was still breathing, as indicated by the bubbles, but to show that he had not completely recovered, Matt gave him a coloring similar to the two other fish that had died. April

Figure
3–11
Matt: "Some died,
and one got sick."

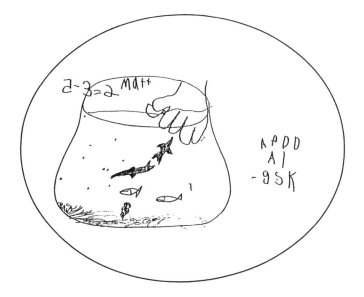

used bubbles to represent her healthy fish and signified her dead fish with a brown color and no bubbles (Figure 3–12).

Both of these children adopted the use of bubbles from an article about beta fish that Tim had read to them in a *Ranger Rick* magazine the week before. Some of the illustrations for the article included photographs of fish with accompanying bubbles. April and Matt remembered this part of the text and tied their knowledge of this past text to a new context in order to solve their current problem.

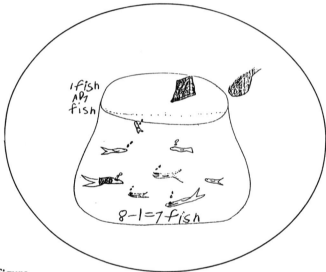

Figure 3–12

April: "One fish and seven fish."

Matt and April were also able to enhance the meaning of this subtraction situation by including a picture of a net that was being lowered into the tank. Every time a fish died in the class tank, Tim would scoop it out with a net. Perhaps the incorporation of this detail helped to reinforce the subsequent tragedy of their stories. April even included a drawing of a plastic bag floating in the top of her bowl, anticipating the arrival of some new fish to replace those that had died. By organizing these details into a coherent whole the children were able to expand the communication potential of their story.

As the children used art, mathematics, and written and oral language to tell their stories, they tried to make sure that all of these communication systems worked in concert to create a unified meaning. The availability of multiple sign systems encouraged them to reflect on their work and to be certain that each system was building and extending the intended meaning of their story. Frequently they would revise their stories so that their message would be consistent across sign systems. Ricky had written, "4 − 1 = 3   1 died" on his paper and went to share it with his teacher. After he had read it Tim noticed an extra fish at the top of his drawing and asked, "What about this fish?"

Ricky paused, looked at his picture intently, and replied, "Oh, I guess I forgot about him!" He counted the fish once more, touching each one as he said the numbers aloud. Then, just before he wrote the numeral 5, he checked the total once more, but in a more efficient manner. He saw the group of four fish at the bottom of his paper and counted that as "four" immediately; he then counted the last fish and said, "five." It is important for children to be able to recognize groups of three, four, and five objects at a glance so that their counting can be more efficient. Ricky was developing this strategy quite naturally through opportunities to use numbers to tell his stories and convey his observations of the world. After rewriting his equation as 5 − 2 = 3, he examined his written statement and realized that it also had to be revised (Figure 3–13).

**Figure
3–13
Ricky: "Two died.
5 − 2 = 3."**

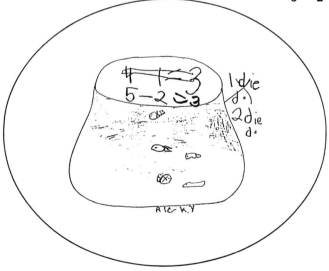

Ricky's willingness to revise demonstrated a healthy attitude about himself as a writer and thinker. Mistakes were not something to be ashamed of; rather they were opportunities to unify all elements of his story. And it was his story. He owned it from the very start. When children are given control for making the decisions, they invest more interest in the process and are more eager to see that the story is clear and well organized.

Jason also worked to revise his story. He had written $10 - 8 = 1$ to accompany his story (Figure 3–14). When Tim asked Jason to explain what his numbers meant, Jason repeated the same story. Tim went to get ten blocks and placed them in front of Jason.

**Figure
3–14**
Jason: "It was ten fish,
and eight died,
and it was one."

"Can you use these to tell me your story?" Tim asked.

"Sure." Jason immediately gathered them together, made two sets of five, and began his story again.

"That's ten. Now see," he said, "There's ten fish and eight die." At this point he pushed eight cubes away and continued. "Then one more dies," he said, pointing to his drawing of a fish that he had colored in black, "and so there's just one left."

"Oh, I see," Tim replied. "I didn't know that another fish had died. How can you use numbers to show the rest of your story?"

He wrote $10 - 8 = 2$, then paused and said, "I can write a 1 next, can't I?"

"If that's what you want to say," responded Tim. Jason then

rewrote the equation again to show that there was only one fish left in the bowl: $10 - 8 = 2\ 1 = 1$.

"There," said Jason, pointing to each number as he retold his story, "see, there's ten fish, and eight die, so there's two and then one more dies, and so there's one left" (Figure 3–15).

**Figure
3–15
Jason working on his
fish story**

Revising to make clear what the author wants to say is not a phenomenon unique to written language. It is a drive across all communication systems—mathematics, art, music, drama, and so on—to communicate one's meaning more cogently and more forcefully. Jason's drawing had included the full story from the very beginning. By coloring one of the two fish that remained black, he showed that only one fish was alive in the tank. For him $10 - 8 = 1$ made perfect sense because his drawing conveyed the intervening step of $2 - 1 = 1$. When he was challenged to devise a numerical representation for his entire story, his solution was a unique one. Although his final equation was not written in a conventional manner, the marks carried meaning for him by placeholding each aspect of his story. He too was learning about mathematics as a system for conveying the important and meaningful details of stories.

Some of the children created stories that contained several events that occurred over time, and they devised some ingenious ways to represent a multiple sequence of actions through art and mathematics. Raphael used a series of numerals to convey the events of his story: $1 + 2 = 3$, then $2 - 1 = 0$. He began writing the numerals $1 + 2 = 3$ on the right side of the paper and then moved to the left to write $2 + 1 = 0$. When he was asked to explain the meaning of his numbers he told a story (Figure 3–16).

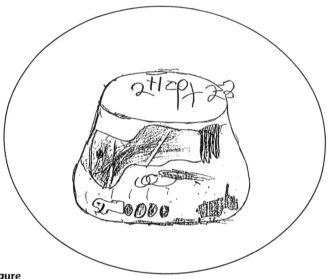

**Figure
3–16**
Raphael: "There was one
fish, and then
one more fish came,
and that's two,
and then one more came,
and that's three.
Then one died,
and that's two,
and then one more died,
and there's one,
and then he died,
and there was zero."

Since Raphael's story was ultimately about three fish that all died, he could have written the equation of $3 - 3 = 0$ to convey his story. However, such an equation would not have represented all the separate events of his story. According to Raphael all of the fish did not enter the tank at the same time nor did they die at the same time. By recording his numerals one at a time he was able to convey each distinct part of the story—that each fish had its own time to enter the tank and its own time to die. He could have recorded the event by writing: $1 + 1 = 2$, $2 + 1 = 3$, $3 - 1 = 2$, $2 - 1 = 1$, $1 - 1 = 0$. By exploring the potential of numbers to represent multiple events over time Raphael is expanding his awareness of the communication potential of the mathematical sign system.

Chris illustrated a similar concept in his work (Figure 3–17). He used art rather than numbers to communicate a series of events that transpired over time. He drew a fish in each of the fish bowls and placed an X on each one to indicate its demise. Thus, Chris chose a different format to convey the separateness of each event. Even though his mathematical equation of $4 - 4 = 0$ would seem to indicate the simultaneous demise

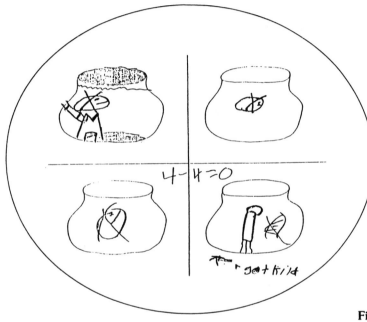

Figure
3–17
Chris: "They all
got killed."

of four fish, Chris's drawings serve to tell the rest of the story. Chris's example shows that a true understanding of any mathematical equation is impossible without considering the total context in which it is placed.

Jesse also chose the format of four fish bowls to tell his story. His description reads from left to right (Figure 3–18). His story recounts the actual event in the classroom when the beta had bitten off part of the black moor's tail. By choosing this particular format Jesse was able to show how the amount of blood poured more profusely as the story proceeded. The first drawing shows the attack; the second drawing illustrates the first bites, which result in some bleeding; the third drawing shows further bleeding as the tail is bitten off; and the last drawing depicts only one fish swimming in the tank, while the other rests at the bottom, encircled by a stream of its own blood. Jesse's numerical representation, $2 - 1 = 1$, reports the final

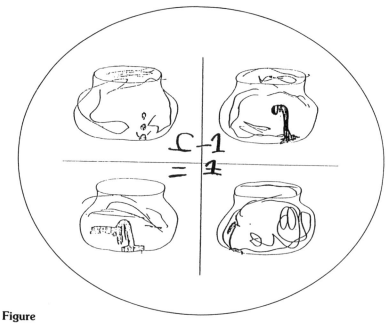

**Figure
3–18**
**Jesse: "He's biting this
one. He's starting
to bleed. He bit his tail off,
and he's eating it.
Blood coming out of his tail."**

outcome but his artistic, written, and verbal descriptions infuse the story with greater detail. Raphael's use of numbers and Chris and Jesse's choice to employ a different format demonstrated for their classmates the various ways that literacy learners can use art, mathematics, and language to convey a series of events that occur over time. They continued to teach each other lessons in how to create meaning.

Although most of the children chose to represent subtraction situations, several portrayed an addition example. Jason found a clever way to represent the joining of two groups through his artwork (Figure 3–19). He drew only part of the fish that was swimming to join the other two. In this way he conveyed how this single fish had "come along" and recently joined the others. Textbooks have difficulty showing this joining of two sets, and children are often confused by the illustrations. However, children grow so much more in their mathematical understanding when they are provided the opportunity to represent that concept themselves. As children shift from one sign system to another, from mathematics to art, they must assume a different stance as learners; they are forced to think in a new way. Their understanding of a concept deepens when they must

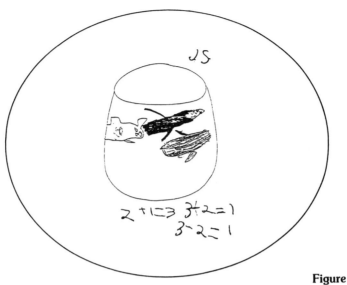

Figure
3–19
Jason: "There were two,
and one came along,
and there were three.
Then two died,
and there was one."

view it from multiple perspectives. Notice also that Jason darkened two fish to show that these two eventually died. He wrote a corresponding equation, $3 - 2 = 1$. Thus, Jason used a drawing of only three fish to convey both an addition and a subtraction story. He cleverly combined two events within the same drawing by using art to show the processes of joining and separating.

As the children worked on their fish stories many talked informally about why some of the fish had died. They shared various reasons that had been discussed at previous class meetings: there was soap in the water; the tank had no filter; there was some kind of poison in the water. Ricky, who had brought a pair of binoculars to school that day and who was examining everything in the room with them—including the fish bowl—offered still another hypothesis when he noticed small pieces of debris in the water: "There's too much trash in the water." Jesse incorporated one of these reasons into the second story that he wrote (Figure 3–20). He took his yellow marker and colored portions of the tank that contained the soap. Jesse used art to lend his story greater detail, which enabled him to demonstrate his knowledge of fish in a more complete way.

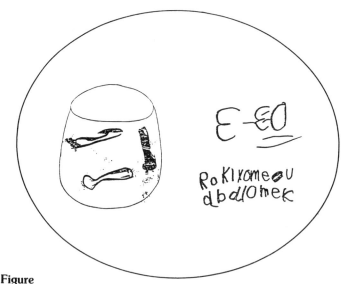

**Figure
3–20**
Jesse: "Three fish died
'cause it had
soap in the tank."

Summary

Through our experience we have seen that building on children's interests can be a powerful way to extend learning in the classroom. In this particular setting, losing teeth and raising fish proved to be themes that the children already knew something about and wanted to pursue further. As they engaged in the process of constructing their stories and sharing their knowledge, they grew as learners of mathematics. They devised ways to use art, mathematics, and language to represent the concepts of addition and subtraction. They used different formats and sign systems to illustrate a series of events that occurred over time. They were provided with opportunities to revise their stories so that their sign systems worked together to convey a unified text. By being asked to clarify their thinking and explain their reasoning the children were challenged to think about their story from another person's perspective. They continued to exploit the diversity of mathematical language to communicate their personal observations. They created some sophisticated mathematical stories that often included multiple events and elaborate detail. Although their numerical marks were not always conventional in form, they were always intentional. All of the children had stories to tell, and they used numbers to enhance the meaning of these stories. In short, they were growing in their understanding of what it means to be truly literate.

Personal Reflection

The questions we posed for ourselves at the beginning of this chapter centered on our concern about whether children would naturally use mathematics to communicate their stories and observations. Their work not only resolved our doubt but also pushed us to reconsider the potential learning opportunities of children constructing their own stories. First, we were struck by the richness of the language that the children used to describe their experiences. The traditional language of textbook story problems, such as "all," "gone," "altogether," "more," and "left," were used by the children in their own stories. We were also surprised at how inventive they were in using art to compress several events into a single drawing. The details they included in their stories caused us to begin to question the importance of labeling certain information in story problems as "irrelevant." The children were helping us see that "irrelevant" is a function of who owns the problem.

The children's work raised some further questions:

1. What are other ways children use drawing to represent the concepts of addition and subtraction?
2. How might children use other communication systems, such as drama or sculpture (clay), to represent mathematical ideas?
3. What are other ways we can set up classroom environments that encourage questioning and observation?
4. How can the children take a more active role not only in sharing their interests but also in collaborating with the teacher to build a curriculum based on those interests?

We were concerned about assuming too much control over their interests. We wanted to involve the children more in discussing and planning how these interests could be extended and explored. We now see it as important to recognize the children as essential collaborators in this curriculum-building process. In this way we can follow the leads of children without distorting their original intent. These questions reflect our growing awareness that children have significant potential for representing mathematical ideas—potential that we had underestimated.

4
EXPLORING MATHEMATICS THROUGH CHILDREN'S LITERATURE

**Quality literature provides
children with a "lived-through"
experience and bears
rereading and reflection.**

**Jerome C. Harste and Kathy G. Short
with Carolyn Burke
Creating Classrooms for Authors**

Children's literature played an important part in this classroom. The children enjoyed story time and incorporated details and characteristics of good literature into their own writing. Tim found that children's literature also created an excellent context for the introduction and exploration of numerical concepts. There are many good examples of literature in which the functional use of numbers is highlighted. In children's literature mathematics is viewed as a process, not merely an event; it is part of a larger experience and can only be understood in its total context. Despite literature's potential for fostering mathematical learning we still had several questions:

1. How can children's literature provide a shared experience from which children can construct their own interpretations?
2. How can literature be used as an invitation to learn about the purposes, processes, and content of the mathematical system?
3. Would the children incorporate group themes (i.e. dinosaurs) or personal themes (i.e. bike riding) into their own stories?
4. How would they coordinate art, mathematics, and written language to convey a unified story?

The children's responses helped us to answer some of these questions and to pose new ones as the school year progressed.

Counting by Twos

It was a balmy spring afternoon. The children had just returned from lunch and were seated on the floor around Tim's story chair. Tim was reading *The Land of Oz* by L. Frank Baum. They had just reached the point in the story where the heroes found themselves trapped in the evil Jackdaw's nest with no obvious way to escape. The children were listening intently. Some were predicting aloud how the heroes might get out of their predicament. Tip, one of the main characters, had recently stumbled upon some magic wishing pills and was reading the instructions: "Directions for Use: Swallow one pill; count to 17 by twos; then make a wish" (1904, p. 208). Tim paused to discuss the concept of counting by twos. He wrote 0 through 20 on the chalkboard and shared a strategy he called skip counting. Starting with 0 he underlined every other number to 20. The children noticed the pattern immediately and began predicting which number would be underlined next. After underlining all of the even numbers it became apparent that the number 17 could not be marked.

"How could they make a wish if they can't get 17?" asked April. Jermaine was quieter than usual. Holding his chin in his hand, he studied the problem.

"They might could just cheat!" exclaimed Rashaun.

Crystal responded, "No, you got to follow the rules. You got to do it right."

The children giggled about this interchange. Jermaine continued to study the number line on the board silently while the others discussed possible solutions to this problem.

Although the children knew the answer lay ahead in the story, they enjoyed such challenges and wanted to exhaust all of the possibilities before Tim continued reading.

Suddenly, Jermaine's eyes widened. He confidently stood up and approached the board. Seeing the confident look on Jermaine's face, Tim anticipated an insightful observation.

"I got it y'all, you just have to start counting with 1. Watch." Instead of beginning with 0 as Tim did, Jermaine pointed to the number 1 and the class helped him skip count until he reached the number 17. Jermaine turned to Tim, grinned, and remarked, "See y'all, I told you so."

Tim continued to read, sharing Baum's slightly different solution. " 'Nevertheless, the creature is right,' declared the Woggle-Bug; 'for twice $\frac{1}{2}$ is one, and if you get to one, it is easy to count from one up to seventeen by twos' " (p. 225).

The children enjoyed hearing another variation to the solution of this counting problem.

The Significance of This Story

Although mathematical investigations were but a small part of Baum's book, Tim capitalized on the opportunity it provided to highlight an important numerical concept. He did so because he believes it is critical to expose children to mathematical ideas through authentic experiences. Counting by twos was naturally embedded in the plot and so offered an effective demonstration of how numbers work in context. The children were also exposed to odd and even number sets, although these were not explicitly treated in this strategy lesson. The children came to value the importance of predicting as a valid and useful way to solve problems. In addition, Jermaine demonstrated that the sign system of mathematics, like language, is open and negotiable, and so he altered Tim's counting strategy in order to try another approach.

Although Tim frequently took advantage of these kinds of instances when mathematics discussions arose spontaneously, he also made a conscious effort to use children's literature, songs, finger plays, and poems that explicitly addressed mathematical concepts. We will show here how Tim integrated three pieces of children's literature with mathematics and encouraged his class to use art, mathematics, and language to communicate their understanding.

Five Little Monkeys

Sometimes, after reading stories that incorporated mathematical ideas, Tim invited the children to make decisions about follow-up experiences. On other occasions, he found that it was important to provide experiences that more specifically addressed concepts he wanted the children to consider. One such example is "Five Little Monkeys."

Tim noticed early in the year that the children enjoyed having personal copies of popular songs and poems. They were useful predictable reading materials. Tim thought that the written version of the popular poem "Five Little Monkeys" might promote literacy learning in the class as well as provide a natural opportunity to demonstrate the meaning of subtraction. Tim's use of the poem also showed how numerals, written language, and illustrations can be used together to create stories.

After sharing the poem together as a class and reading it many times from a large chart posted at the front of the room, the children were invited to make up their own versions. After most of the poem was written on the chalkboard, volunteers completed verses by filling in numbers in blanks left at the beginning of the first two sentences: "_____ little monkeys jumping on the bed. _____ fell off and broke his (their) head(s)." Next, Tim suggested that the children use numbers to help them tell their story and that they draw a picture of the event. The children were given individual copies of the text with blank spaces so that they could create their own stories. We wondered how the children would represent subtraction stories given this format.

Raymond responded by exploring the concept of zero in each of his scenarios. His equations for the stories were $1 - 1 = 0$, $1 - 0 = 1$, and $2 - 2 = 0$. Although zero can be an abstract concept for young children, Raymond showed us that he was ready to explore it. He not only used zero to illustrate a take-away situation, such as $1 - 1 = 0$ and $2 - 2 = 0$, but he also used zero as the subtrahend $(1 - 0 = 1)$ to communicate that one monkey rested comfortably on the bed without bothering to jump off. Obviously, Raymond did not need formal preparation to investigate the meaning of zero. The open-ended structure of this task allowed him to explore these different contexts for zero as he tested his mathematical hypothesis. Harste, Woodward, and Burke (1984) helped us understand that young children learn language efficiently because of their natural desire to think about new language hypotheses. We believe that Raymond's exercise shows that this theory holds true for mathematical literacy as well.

Jermaine chose to investigate something entirely different. He was known to be curious about number patterns and frequently used them to create and solve his own math problems. This day was no exception. Jermaine decreased the minuend in each verse by one and increased the subtrahend by one (Figure 4–1). His three equations,

$$9 - 1 = 8$$
$$8 - 2 = 6$$
$$7 - 3 = 4$$

proved to be an interesting pattern, as well as a vehicle for exploring how changes in an equation affect the answer. In this case Jermaine shows that decreasing the minuend by 1 and increasing the subtrahend by one will result in a difference that will be two less than the previous equation. Number stories written by children have led us to believe that the more opportunities children have to alter a particular problem or equation, the greater their understanding of that operation becomes. Children's literature provides a natural context for this kind of problem posing (Brown and Walter 1983); certain problem attributes can be varied so that other dimensions of the problems can be pursued. Children's number sense is strengthened when they are allowed to poke around with numbers, gaining insight into the relative effects certain changes have on their

**Figure
4–1
Jermaine's monkeys**

solutions (Whitin 1989a). In this spirit of playfulness children can discover important numerical relationships and unique patterns that lurk beneath the surface as they systematically change the problem variables.

This exploration also gave Jermaine a chance to see the role that illustrations play in communicating mathematical messages. In his first story, he drew nine smiling faces to represent the monkeys and then designated the monkey that fell off by excluding it from the group. He was able to devise his own unique way for communicating the concept of subtraction through art. He found this strategy successful and used it in his other two stories.

James also devised ways to communicate this story through art. In his first story James illustrated $4 - 1 = 3$ by appropriately showing three monkeys on a bed with one monkey flying off onto its head. He communicated the movement by drawing arched lines behind the unfortunate one. After favorable comments from his peers, James took this strategy to its extreme by showing $10 - 10 = 0$. Using one-to-one correspondence, he used arched lines to portray the action of all ten monkeys falling off the bed. As James considered his third story, he noticed that there was very little space at the end of the page. To solve this problem he simply decided to write $0 - 0 = 0$ (Figure 4–2). The limited amount of space available prompted him nevertheless to devise an appropriate mathematical problem.

Ernie also used art to tell his story. His illustrations differed from many of the others in the class because they did not explicitly represent the numbers in his stories. Instead, his artwork communicated the general idea of the text. While other children used their pictures to help solve their problems, Ernie relied on a strategy he found successful in other subtraction contexts. He drew sets of circles to indicate the minuend in each of his story problems. After reading each written text, he crossed out the appropriate number of objects indicated by the subtrahend. He calculated the answers by counting the remaining objects and wrote an equation for each story (Figure 4–3).

Round as a Pancake

Like all teachers, Tim had to work within certain district guidelines and objectives. One of the materials available to him to meet these objectives was a mathematics workbook. Although he knew that these books covered the material set forth by the district guidelines, he believed that his role as a teacher was one of uncovering, rather than merely covering, mathematical principles. For this reason, Tim felt that experiences should be open-ended, spark an interest in the children, foster originality, and encourage dialogue among the community of learners. Therefore, he developed a strategy using children's literature that allowed the class to connect their past experiences to their current understanding of number sets.

Tim reminded the children of the number of books they had made that were patterned after *Anno's Counting Book* (Anno 1977). He told them he was going to read another mathematical story, which focused on round objects. The children would then be invited to create their own books using numbers like those in the counting book and round shapes like those in "Round as a Pancake" (Sullivan 1972).

After listening to the story, the children began suggesting objects in the classroom that were round.

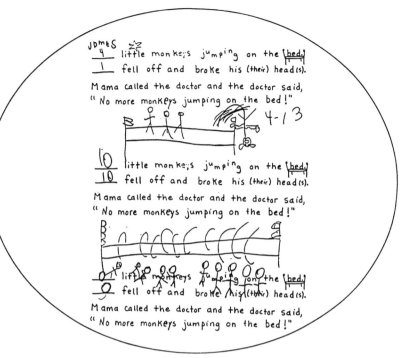

James

___4___ little monkeys jumping on the {bed}
___1___ fell off and broke his (their) head(s).
Mama called the doctor and the doctor said,
" No more monkeys jumping on the bed !"

4-13

___10___ little monkeys jumping on the {bed}
___10___ fell off and broke his (their) head(s).
Mama called the doctor and the doctor said,
" No more monkeys jumping on the bed !"

___0___ little monkeys jumping on the {bed}
___0___ fell off and broke his (their) head(s).
Mama called the doctor and the doctor said,
" No more monkeys jumping on the bed !"

**Figure
4–2
James: 0 – 0 = 0**

Ernie

___10___ little monkeys jumping on the {bed}
___7___ fell off and broke his (their) head(s).
Mama called the doctor and the doctor said,
" No more monkeys jumping on the bed !"

10 - 7 = 3

___8___ little monkeys jumping on the {bed}
___1___ fell off and broke his (their) head(s).
Mama called the doctor and the doctor said,
" No more monkeys jumping on the bed !"

8 - 1 = 7

___9___ little monkeys jumping on the {bed}
___6___ fell off and broke his (their) head(s).
Mama called the doctor and the doctor said,
" No more monkeys jumping on the bed !"

9 - 6 = 3

**Figure
4–3
Ernie uses art to tell
his number story**

"That clock is round," suggested Shamarla. There was a murmur of agreement while the others searched the room.

"How about the masking tape?" offered Ernie.

Jason said, "The chalk is round."

The conversation continued as most of the children made contributions to this list.

Next, the children were supplied with blank books and plenty of round, colored stickers. Tim suggested they create their own shape-number books. He told them that they could use ideas from other books or create their own content. He also reminded them that the number and color words were posted in the room. As usual, the children's creations were often more interesting than the original published texts.

Crystal began her book by making one balloon, two suns, and three spiders. On page four she expanded the simple numbering of sets by placing four red dots in a rectangular pattern and connecting them with a thin blue line. She approached page five in a similar way but varied the colors by using three red dots and two green ones. Again, she connected the dots and made a pentagon (Figure 4–4). All the time she

**Figure
4–4**

**Crystal: "Connect the dots,
la, la, la . . ."**

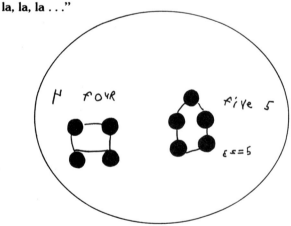

was working on these pages, she sang, "Connect the dots, la, la, la. . . ." When Tim asked about her book Crystal responded, "This is like Pee-Wee Herman. He connects the dots one, two, three, four." Then she sang the song again.

Next, Crystal explained her number sentence, 3 2 = 5. "You can say two and three or three and two make five." Crystal's number sentence reflects the colored subsets she used to make the number five. She used three red dots and two green dots. Her explanation showed that she understood the commutative property of addition because she confidently interchanged the addends knowing that the sum would remain the same.

Tim smiled at Crystal's song and the way she used color to show the meaning of her number sentence. He was especially pleased that Crystal moved beyond the stories presented in class to create an original text. Crystal connected this experience with her favorite Saturday morning television show. This strategy helped her make sense of the current experience in light of past ones.

Ernie also made a connection with past texts by drawing upon his knowledge of fairy tales. On page two of Ernie's book he placed two green dots side by side. He drew a queen complete with crown out of the first dot and a flower with stem and petals from the second (Figure 4–5). "This is a queen or a

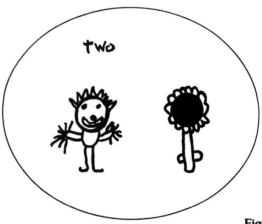

**Figure
4–5**
**Ernie: "This is a queen
or a princess,
and she is picking a flower
for her king."**

princess, and she is picking a flower for her king," Ernie remarked when describing his page. Although neither of the two example books used fairy tale structure or language, Ernie chose to use a fairy tale theme to extend his numerical task. Other children in the class reacted favorably to his story line, thereby reinforcing the importance of taking risks to write unique, personally meaningful stories. Ernie enjoyed fairy tales and integrated content from such stories frequently across various learning experiences. These important links between familiar children's literature and classroom learning experiences were made through conversation, demonstrations, and opportunities to construct his own texts.

On page six of Chris's book, he drew upon his knowledge of dinosaurs from the recently completed dinosaur unit to classify his set of six (Figure 4–6).

"Three plant eaters and three meat eaters, that's six," Chris explained. His understanding of dinosaurs was evident in his accurate depiction of the differences between plant eaters and

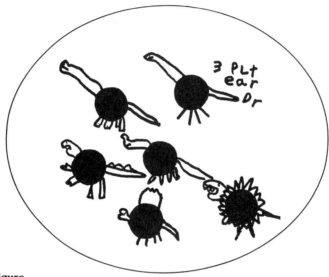

**Figure
4–6**
**Chris's set of six:
Three plant eaters
and three meat eaters**

meat eaters. All of his plant eaters stood on four legs, while the meat eaters walked on their hind legs (with the exception of dimetrodon, who was one of the only true meat eaters to walk on four legs). Chris supported his pictorial text by writing, "3 plt ear dr" (three plant-eater dinosaurs). When the class shared their books at gathering, Tim asked Chris, "Can you think of an easy way to add these up?"

"Just count the plant eaters and the meat eaters, they make six." Chris used his classification scheme to add efficiently. While learning mathematics, Chris was obviously using math to learn and to share his knowledge with others.

Jermaine also extended the dinosaur unit by incorporating these prehistoric reptiles into his book. On page six, he used three different colors to represent his dinosaurs: two blue, two green, and two red. In addition to writing the number word

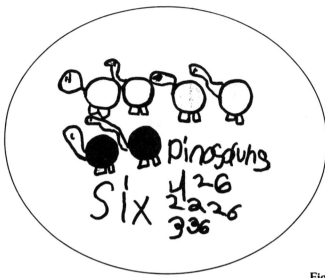

**Figure
4–7**
**Jermaine's set of six:
Six dinosaurs**

for 6, he wrote "dinosaurs" to label his illustrations (Figure
4–7).

When asked about an easy way to add his creatures, Jermaine smiled and answered, "Two and two and two makes
six." He pointed to each color subset as he spoke. "And you
could do four and two," referring to the top row of four and
the second row of two.

"Are there any other ways?" Tim asked.

Jermaine contemplated this question for a moment before
answering, "Yeah, three and three."

As he developed each number sentence, he wrote it carefully: 2 2 2 6, 3 3 6 and 4 2 6. While he omitted the conventional
addition and equal symbols, his explanation made his meaning
clear.

Since this experience was open-ended, Jermaine was able
to create a counting book that challenged his current understanding of the mathematical system. His investigation into
names for 6 provided him an important insight into this system.
Numbers do have various names, and learners need to be able
to use these names flexibly to meet the demands of certain
problems. When doing the problem $42 - 17$ children learn
to rename 42 as $30 + 12$ in order to exchange. When children
add fractions with unlike denominators, such as $\frac{1}{2} + \frac{5}{6}$, they
learn to rename $\frac{1}{2}$ as $\frac{3}{6}$. Jermaine's investigations emphasized
the importance of this principle of renaming.

Seven Eggs

The children had studied animals in September and October but continued to show an active interest in them throughout the year. Tim drew on this strong interest whenever possible by integrating animals into other learning experiences and projects. Throughout the year the children and Tim continued to expand and refine their knowledge of and appreciation for animals. Tim developed the following strategy to let the children again use numbers for a real purpose as they continued to explore the animal kingdom.

Tim began by reading *Seven Eggs* (Hooper 1985). Since it was a predictable book, he invited the children to join in whenever they wanted. Several children responded immediately. Others watched and listened as the story unfolded. Tim paused at highly predictable points in the text to give the children a chance to read independently. By midstory almost everyone was reading in chorus.

Next, Tim shared books and magazine articles that described the various sizes and colors of animals' eggs and places where they lay them. Then the class generated a list of animals, including snakes, turtles, fish, birds, and dinosaurs, that lay eggs.

The discussion that followed helped the children use their knowledge of dinosaurs and animals. The children were then asked to create their own mathematical stories using what they knew about egg-laying animals. Round colored stickers, paper, and art supplies were made available. The children's diverse creations showed a sophisticated understanding of both mathematical concepts and animal behavior (Figure 4–8).

All of the children naturally integrated science, language, and mathematics by accurately depicting situations in which animals lay eggs. Rashaun said during the class discussion that some animals die while giving birth. He then presented this understanding in his story (Figure 4–9). In Rashaun's first example he told us that the alligator died because her babies were coming out. In his second example, Rashaun explained another animal fact by noting that cobra snakes lay eggs.

When Raphael was retelling his story about dinosaurs eating each other's eggs, he attached a different dinosaur name to each egg. Brontosaurus, duckbill, and dimetrodon were all used to signify the various dinosaurs in his story.

Matt and Chris were sensitive to the location that animals used to lay their eggs. In his first story Matt showed four eggs

**Figure
4–8
Jesse creating an egg story**

**Figure
4–9
Rashaun: "The alligator died
because her babies
were coming out."**

hatching at different periods of time, since he drew some dinosaurs larger than others. In Matt's second story he carefully placed each egg in a hole in the ground for protection (Figure 4–10) and depicted one of the five hatching, recording the story as $5 - 1 = 4$. Likewise, Chris placed his unhatched turtle eggs under the sand, next to the ocean. The emerging

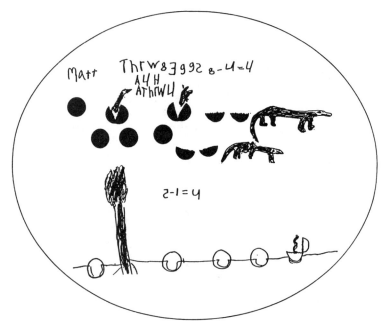

**Figure
4–10**

Matt: "There were eight eggs and
four hatched.
And there were four.
$8 - 4 = 4$
$5 - 1 = 4$"

**Figure
4–11**

Chris: "We had three.
One hatched;
there were two left.
We had two.
Then one hatched.
Then there were one left."

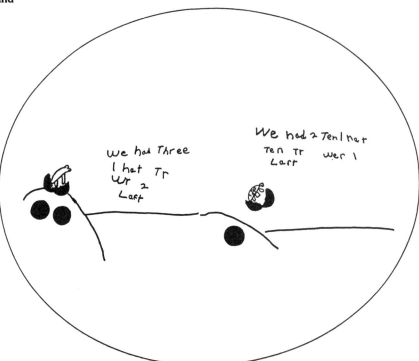

sea turtles were drawn above ground about to begin their trek to the ocean (Figure 4–11). In addition to showing what they knew about animals, both authors used the different sign systems of art, mathematics, and language to construct and share their meaning. Their drawings, written texts, and use of numbers in combination communicated their ideas effectively.

Like Chris and Matt, Katie used several means to convey her message (Figure 4–12). When reading her text, "The frog

Figure 4–12
Katie: "The frog popped out of his egg.
There's three eggs left."

popped out of his egg. There's three eggs left," she used terminology traditionally associated with subtraction word problems. Her equation of $1 + 3$ demonstrates the set-within-a-set situation for subtraction. There is no take-away or comparison made here. Instead there is merely a description of a set of four eggs, one of which has hatched and three others that remain unhatched. Of the total set of four, there is a subset of hatched (one) and unhatched (three) eggs. One and three can be described as complements of the same set. Here again children can explore these different circumstances for subtraction when they have opportunities to tie them to experiences that are relevant to them.

Typically, mathematics textbooks have suggested that we restrict beginning addition and subtraction story problems to single operations. Two-step problems have often been considered complex and confusing. Jason showed us, however, that

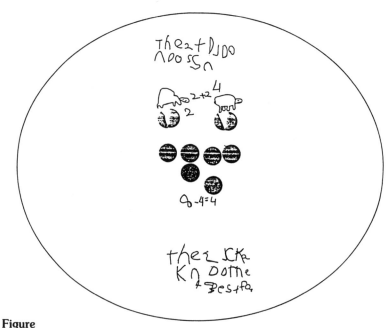

Figure 4–13
Jason: "There was two turtles
headed for the ocean.
Then two other eggs
were cracking.
Then four eggs were left."

when tasks are open-ended children will set their own challenges and go beyond traditional assumptions about learning.

In Jason's story about sea turtles, he began with eight eggs: two hatched, two cracked, and four intact. In invented spelling Jason wrote, "There was two turtles headed for the ocean. Then two other eggs were cracking. Then four eggs were left" (Figure 4–13). To signify the fact that two eggs had hatched, Jason carefully illustrated two turtles rising above their opened eggs, heading toward the blue ocean on the right side of his paper. Jason cut two other eggs with scissors to designate those that were still cracking. After sticking these on his paper he wrote 2 + 2 4. Next, Jason placed the four remaining stickers on his paper and determined the total number of eggs to be eight. Finally, he wrote the equation $8 - 4 = 4$. This equation represented the total number of eggs minus the two that had hatched and the two that were still cracking. Conventionally, one might write this entire problem as $8 - (2 + 2) = 4$. While Jason did not use this single equation, he showed the same meaning in his own way.

Summary

By using children's literature as a basis for exploring mathematical concepts, Tim provided experiences for the children in this class from which they could construct and share their own interpretations (Figure 4–14).

**Figure
4–14
Ricky and Raphael
compare dinosaurs**

The students used children's literature as a medium for exploring a variety of mathematical principles: number patterns, the concept of zero, situations for addition and subtraction, one-to-one correspondence, shapes, the commutative property of addition, and two-step story problems. These explorations demonstrate the open-ended potential of children's literature as a means for discovering important mathematical principles.

Personal Reflection

Excited about the potential of using children's literature to extend mathematical learning, we asked ourselves a new set of questions:

1. What other mathematical books are there that can be tied to popular themes of study? We felt that children's literature provided an important springboard for children to generate their own stories and wanted to find other resources to use.
2. What strategies would children demonstrate if they responded to these stories using other communication systems, such as drama or clay?
3. What are the characteristics of children's literature that would

indicate its potential for teaching mathematical concepts?

4. What are other ways that teachers can involve children in discovering mathematical insights that are embedded in children's literature?

5. How can children's literature be used more effectively as a vehicle for unifying the curriculum?

5
EXPLORING
THE POTENTIAL
OF GRAPHING

Are we drowning in digits?
Is the end in sight?
Yes we are, and no it is not.

Philip Davis and Reuben Hersh
The World According to Descartes

We live in an age in which graphs and charts play a significant role. Every magazine or newspaper we pick up displays some kind of graphic information. Companies fill their advertisements and commercials with the latest statistical evidence to convince us that now is the time to buy their products. We are inundated with questionnaires, phone calls, and surveys to determine our particular preferences. This incessant barrage of preference probing affects what we eat, what we wear, what we drive, what we see on television, and the way we spend our money. Political surveys gather information on voter preference; television ratings document the viewing habits of the general populace; advertising people use surveys to gather data about the feelings, customs, and habits of different groups of people. Thus, graphs are an integral part of the way we communicate with each other. To become informed citizens and consumers, children need regular opportunities to gather information in order to make decisions or solve problems; they need to use graphs to help them organize their information and interpret their results.

We were intrigued by the potential for learning that graphs and surveys had for children. We thought that graphs could be a vehicle for integrating writing, drawing, and mathematics. However, we were still uncertain how children would use and construct graphs. Therefore, we asked ourselves these questions at the outset:

1. What different ways will children use to record their information?
2. What kind of interpretations will children be able to make of their data?
3. What kind of learning will take place as children interact with each other during the course of their survey?
4. How can we help children learn basic mathematical concepts through graphing?
5. How can we help children appreciate the diversity in content and form that graphing takes?
6. How can graphs be integrated into the daily life of the classroom?

Previously, as classroom teachers, we had used graphs without connecting them to curricular themes or personal interests. We knew that graphs and surveys encouraged a lot of social interaction and were anxious to see how the children would share insights with each other about their questions as well as their interpretations.

Strategies for Using Graphs with Young Children

The children in this transition classroom used graphs and personal surveys throughout the year. They used them for many reasons in various situations. For the sake of clarity, we have divided the graphing experiences that children encountered into four categories:

1. Integrating graphs into the daily life of the classroom.
2. Encouraging personal surveys.
3. Constructing graphs to make classroom decisions.
4. Using graphs to learn.

These categories are not in any way meant to be mutually exclusive. Instead, they highlight the diversity of graphing experiences and demonstrate the rich potential that graphs afford children for sharing and extending their learning. The children learn graphing as they explore how and under what conditions people use graphs. They also learn about graphing as they investigate different formats for recording their information. They learn through graphing as they discover how to interpret their results and choose graphing procedures that best meet their needs. As children explore all three facets they gain a deeper and broader understanding of the potential graphing holds as a vehicle for explaining and exploring their social world (Figure 5–1).

Integrating Graphs into the Daily Life of the Classroom

On several occasions during the year the children decided which of several books they enjoyed the most. One day in October they were presented with a graph listing three choices of Halloween stories: *Georgie* by Robert Bright, *Clifford's Halloween* by Norman Bridwell, and *It Didn't Frighten Me* by Janet Goss and Jerome Harste (Figure 5–2). As Jermaine wrote his name on the graph, he looked at Rashaun's name. He then counted the number of letters in each name.

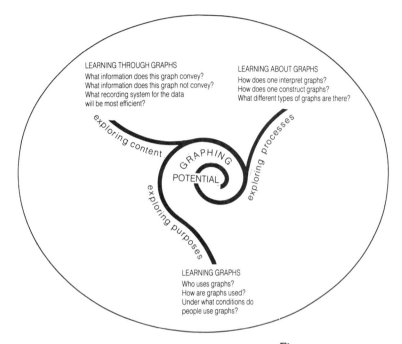

LEARNING THROUGH GRAPHS
What information does this graph convey?
What information does this graph not convey?
What recording system for the data
will be most efficient?

LEARNING ABOUT GRAPHS
How does one interpret graphs?
How does one construct graphs?
What different types of graphs are there?

exploring content

GRAPHING
POTENTIAL

exploring processes

exploring purposes

LEARNING GRAPHS
Who uses graphs?
How are graphs used?
Under what conditions do
people use graphs?

**Figure
5–1
The potential of graphs**

**Figure
5–2
Which book do you
like best?**

"What do you notice?" Tim asked.

"My name is longer," he replied.

Jesse had been observing this interaction. He then wrote his name on the graph and began to look at the other names. He counted the letters in his name, paused, and then counted the letters in "Chris."

"Hey, they're the same!" he exclaimed. He continued to count the letters in other names; he discovered some, such as Daehoon, were longer than his, but found several others, such as April and James, that were the same length.

This story demonstrates how children can learn through mathematics as they devise their own unique mathematical extensions to a given experience. Even though the intent of the graph was not to record the lengths of first names, the children noticed this possibility and took the initiative to explore it. Ever since school had begun they had shown a keen interest in each other's names. They often recorded classmates' names in their journals and were learning to recognize each other's names on the sign-in sheet that they used each morning to record the daily attendance. Thus, this numerical investigation was merely a natural extension of a topic that had already generated a lot of enthusiasm.

Jermaine's comment, "My name is longer," illustrates his intent to use numbers for comparison. Mathematics is a language that contains many words that describe relationships: longer, shorter, equal, heavier, lighter, faster, smaller, and so on. Children learn about mathematics as they use language to describe their observations in relational terms. Mathematics is a system for showing relationships, and children gain insight into this dimension of the system as they communicate their findings with each other.

As Jesse scanned the graph he was eager to find names that were composed of the same number of letters as his own. Once he found "Chris" he eagerly sought out some more. He kept estimating which names looked to be of equal length, and he then counted to confirm his prediction. If his choice was too long, such as Daehoon, he would revise his notion of an appropriate length and try again. There was no one there to tell him if he was right or wrong. Instead, Jesse monitored his own estimates, made adjustments, and continued to make further predictions. Estimation is a crucial mathematical skill and Jesse used it quite naturally, on his own initiative, because he was pursuing a question that was interesting to him. Some studies show that eighty percent of the mathematics people do on a daily basis is related to estimation and mental computation (Reys 1986). However, for many years schools have neglected this purposeful dimension of mathematics. The focus has been on right answers only. Estimation is an important aspect of mathematical literacy because it encourages risk taking and promotes flexible thinking. The open nature of this graphing experience provided Jesse the opportunity to estimate, predict, and explore the length of words in his own way.

At another time during the year Tim had read the children many stories by Dr. Seuss. The children constructed a class graph to determine which of three books was the most popular: *The 500 Hats of Bartholomew Cubbins, Hop on Pop*, and *One Fish, Two Fish, Red Fish, Blue Fish*. After they noted their preferences, Tim invited the children to record on a separate piece of paper something they had discovered in making this graph. Normally the children discussed the graph together; however, Tim felt that on this day it might be interesting to view the written observations that the children made on their own.

The children wrote a variety of responses. April and Jermaine's personal interpretations of the data show how children can learn through mathematics. April wrote a numerical statement: "500 Hats has 9." She had tallied one of the columns and wrote the total for her answer (Figure 5–3).

Jermaine wrote a different kind of numerical response: "Red

**Figure
5–3
April: "500 hats has 9."**

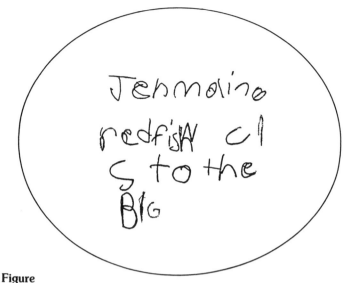

fish is closest to the biggest'' (Figure 5–4). Although Jermaine's statement contains no numbers, it demonstrates that he noted a numerical relationship. He compared two columns and found which one came closest to the most popular choice. His use of the words "closest" and "biggest" illustrates again how children can use the language of mathematics in a natural way to share personal observations.

Rashaun did use numbers to record his observation. However, his particular response demonstrated his decision to learn more about the mathematics system itself. He wrote: "I like 5000000000000." He is not only stating his preference but also testing out what he knows about large numbers (Figure

5–5). He knew that the story contained an enormous number of hats and he used a long series of 0's to signify that large quantity. His response is enlightening for several reasons. First, he demonstrates a beginning understanding of place value, showing that the more digits a number has, the larger the number will be. Second, he demonstrates a sensitivity to the context of zero. The number he chose to repeat twelve times was zero. Even though he could see from the graph that five hundred was composed of two zeros, he could have chosen to extend it using other numerals. However, if one looks closely at the large numbers reported in newspapers and magazines, they are usually rounded off with zeros so that they will be more convenient and easier to remember. A school budget of $489,627 is usually reported as $500,000. The annual budget of the United States was recently reported as $1,000,000,000. Thus, Rashaun was learning about the system of mathematics as he tested out what he knew about the concept of place value and the significance of zero as a sign for large numbers.

Other children chose not to record a numerical statement but to provide additional information about one of the stories. One child used four different colors to write "Blue fish, green fish, orange fish, and purple fish." He used a different color for each line and used art to emphasize the fact that this book portrayed fish of many colors. Jesse wrote, "I like *Hop on Pop* because it rhymes" (Figure 5–6).

**Figure
5–6**
**Jesse: "I like *Hop on Pop*
because it rhymes."**

Ernie wrote, "*Hop on Pop* Dr. Seuss," including the author's name as a way to make his choice more detailed and complete. In these ways the children used this written invitation to extend what they had recorded initially. On the typical class graph they could only sign their name; now they could share additional information they found relevant—the colors of the fish, the rhyming scheme, and the author's name. The children were learning through mathematics that graphs provide a concise yet restrictive form for displaying information. Although graphs are a succinct vehicle for conveying an abundance of numerical data, they do not tell the whole story. The written responses of the children provided additional information about the books that was not included on their graph.

Other children chose to elaborate on their personal preferences. Katie wrote, "I like the *500 Hats* because it was the best"; Shamarla wrote, "I like all the books" (Figure 5–7).

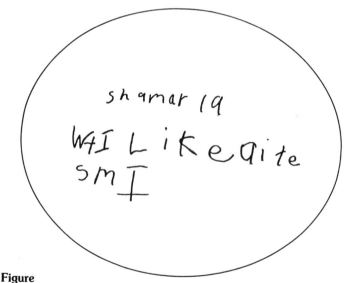

**Figure
5–7**
Shamarla: "I like all the books."

Shamarla felt restricted by being able to write her name only once; she wanted to explain that she had enjoyed all the books. This written invitation allowed her to share her thinking with her peers. Her response underscored for the class that graphs are limited in what they can tell us. The degree of personal conviction that a child held for any given choice was not indicated on the graph. No differentiation was made among strong, mild, and tentative preferences; all were counted to be the same. Children need opportunities to analyze graphs to determine the kind of information graphs can and cannot provide.

The children were also learning through graphing as they confronted the issue of voting for more than one choice. In early graphing experience on favorite fruits, Katie voted for two of the choices. When questioned about this tactic during a class discussion, she defended her strategy by saying, "My first name likes bananas and my last name likes grapes!" Despite her clever justification most children insisted that each person ought to be restricted to one choice; they claimed that some people might try to cheat and write their name many times so that a particular choice would win. Nevertheless, depending on the survey, there were still some children who would occasionally vote for more than one choice. Although the discussion never really resolved the issue, it was important because it helped to highlight for the children another question surrounding the construction of graphs. There are times when people are requested to vote for more than one choice—when electing members of the board of trustees at a particular college, for example, or when responding to marketing surveys that request people to indicate several reasons why they shop at a particular store. Thus, the issue that the children were debating was a significant one because it provided them the opportunity to explore more fully the different contexts of graphing. They were motivated to pursue this particular question because it grew out of a mathematical investigation that they had initiated and carried out. This issue also arose because children had the opportunity to interact with each other. Since everyone had cast a vote, they all felt a certain ownership of the graph's creation, and they were persistent in challenging each other to justify their diverse decisions. The important point here is not that the issue was settled, but that the question arose, and that the children were provided the time to explore it, thereby growing in their appreciation for the communication potential of graphing. It is this growth that is at the heart of mathematical literacy.

Encouraging Personal Surveys

DO YOU KNOW HOW TO FIX BIKES?

"Hey, you want to know what I got?" asked Matt as he walked into school one morning in April.

"Yes, I'd like to know," Tim said. "Tell me about it."

"I got a BMX. It's a bike, and I can do tricks on it," he replied. Matt continued to explain the tricks he could perform. After a while Tim said, "Matt, you certainly know a lot about bikes. You might want to go around the room and ask a question about bikes to the rest of the class."

Matt cocked his head, thought for a few seconds, and then exclaimed, "Hey, I know. I'll ask 'em, 'Do you know how to fix bikes?' "

"That sounds like an interesting question," said Tim. "What do you suppose you're going to find out?"

"I don't know," he replied.

"Make a guess," Tim requested. "What do you think you will discover after you have asked everyone your question?"

"I don't think they know how to fix bikes," he said.

"Oh, you think most people don't know how to fix bikes. Well, start your survey, and let's see what you find out."

Tim supported Matt in taking a risk and making a prediction. Just as in writing, this risk taking is an important facet of mathematical literacy. Numbers are often used to investigate a hunch or support an inkling. By making a prediction Matt set a focus for his query. He sought to confirm the outcome he had anticipated, and this intent was obvious as he walked about the room during his investigation. He was involved in the process of learning mathematics by broadening his understanding of the role that surveys play in generating further information about a topic of personal significance. After he had tallied several responses, he would pause, scan his survey sheet, and then count to determine the total for each category. After he had completed the first column of responses on the left, he could tell by merely scanning the results that the "no's" represented the majority of voters (Figure 5–8). As he completed the rest of the survey he did not bother to count the responses any longer. He could tell which reply was going to be most prevalent, and that was the only issue that mattered. Thus, Matt changed his counting strategy as more and more votes were tallied. Initially he counted the total votes for "yes" and "no" after sets of two or three votes were cast. However, as the result became more obvious, he merely scanned his recording sheet, estimating whether or not the "no" votes were still in the majority.

In constructing his graph Matt drew a bicycle first at the

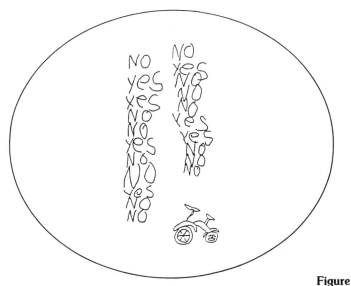

Figure
5–8
Matt's survey: "Do you know
how to fix bikes?"

bottom of his paper. He then surveyed his classmates, recording their responses with a "yes" or a "no." He had no specific
column for each response; rather, he recorded each vote in
the order in which it was given to him. Several times during
his survey the children would not reply merely with a "yes"
or "no" but would clarify their expertise. Raymond said, "I
can fix it a little"; Jermaine explained, "I don't know how to
fix all of it, but I know how to fix the wheels." Matt tallied their
responses as "no." However, when Matt shared with the class
the results of his survey later on in the morning, this issue of
experience was raised again. Children with no experience re-
pairing bikes were placed in the same category with those who
could fix wheels or adjust a seat. It was not a homogeneous
group, but the manner in which Matt recorded their responses
did not differentiate among the diverse kinds of experience that
the children had. Matt had to listen and decide how to interpret
each child's response. According to his definition, someone
who could not repair all aspects of bikes was assigned a "no"
classification on the survey.

   Matt's query differed sharply from some other surveys the
children had completed. During their study of animals the children had responded to such questions as "Do you have a cat?"
or "Do you have a dog?" The results of these surveys seemed
more definitive. Matt's survey did not reflect the various gra-

dations of responses. The important point to be made here is that Matt's survey and the class discussion that followed helped to expand the children's awareness of the communication potential of certain types of graphs. They were learning through graphs that, depending on the question that is asked, some graphs cannot represent the subtle variations of replies. The children were also learning that some kinds of information are not conveyed by graphs. Jermaine, Raymond, and others expressed this concern by claiming that their limited experience with bikes was not indicated in any way on Matt's graph. Their remarks were helping to develop in all the children a healthier respect for numerical information. Such sensitivity is crucial if children are to be informed and enlightened examiners of numerical information.

During the class discussion children were eager to hear about Matt's results.

"How many said 'yes'?" they inquired. Matt counted and said "seven". Matt's communication of his findings demonstrated for his fellow classmates one of the purposes of mathematics. Surveys are vehicles for extending our knowledge of particular subjects and for answering questions of personal significance.

"How many said 'no'?" asked Joyce. As Matt was counting his responses, Jermaine piped up, "Eleven. It has to be eleven, because there's eighteen in the class." Although his response was not quite accurate because Matt had also surveyed all the adults in the room, Jermaine still provided the class with a unique insight into his thinking. First, he took a risk by predicting what the total would be without looking at the survey himself. Numbers are often embedded in situations that encourage such predicting. One of the situations in which subtraction arises is known as the "missing addend." Jermaine used this context for subtraction to solve his problem. He reasoned: "$7 + \square = 18$." He knew one addend and the sum and sought to find the other addend. Such problems can often be difficult for children because the inclusion of the plus sign makes them appear to be addition problems. Children often add 7 and 18 to find their answer, since those are the only two available numbers to add. Jermaine demonstrated a good understanding of this missing-addend situation. His investigation into this subtraction problem illustrates how children can

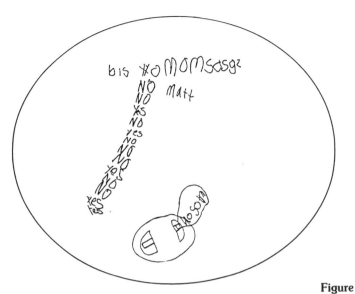

learn about mathematics when they are engaged in meaningful literacy endeavors.

DOES YOUR MOM SMOKE CIGARETTES?

On a Friday morning during free-choice time Matt decided to find out how many children's mothers smoked cigarettes. When asked why he chose this topic Matt replied, "'Cause my mom smokes and I told her to quit so she won't get black lungs." (A few weeks earlier the class had seen an animated film on smoking presented by the guidance counselor. Matt found the film interesting and informative, and he decided to share his knowledge and concern with his family.) Again, Matt was demonstrating the purposes of mathematics as he addressed an important personal query through a survey.

With markers and paper Matt was ready to start creating his survey. He began by making what looked like a backwards capital D on the bottom left part of his paper. From this mark he ingeniously created the international symbol for "no smoking," complete with a lit cigarette and smoke coming from the tip. At this point Matt was interested in exploring the processes used to send his message. His orchestration of art and written language gave his survey a richer meaning. "I'd better do some writing too," he said to himself. Protruding from the end of the cigarette, in a cloud of smoke, Matt wrote NO SOKN (no smoking). At the top of the page he wrote his question (Figure 5–9): DIS XYO MOM SO SGS (Does your mom smoke cigarettes?). When he came to the y for *your* he looked up at the alphabet on the wall and proceeded to write an x. "I made a x instead of a y. Oh well," he said and continued writing the question in his invented spelling. It was clear he did not want to be distracted from his larger concern of canvassing his peers to ascertain the smoking behavior of their mothers. When he was ready, he started around the room, asking his question and recording answers with a "yes" or "no" on his paper in a single column. Matt went far beyond the mere mathematical dimension of this task by including art and written language to create his survey (Figure 5–10).

Figure
5–10
Matt conducting his survey

Chris answered Matt's survey question by saying, "My mommy doesn't smoke but my daddy does." "I'm just asking about your mom," answered Matt. He recorded a "no" and moved on to his next respondent. This interaction spurred Chris to generate more information on this topic. He walked to the writing center and started to create his own survey: DUS YOUR DADDY SOK (Does your daddy smoke?). The way in which

Chris extended Matt's original idea emphasizes again the social nature of learning (Figure 5–11). Chris, too, was exploring the purposes of mathematics: He was learning that he could modify the original question so that he could pursue another facet of it that was more interesting to him. Children investigate the purposes of mathematics together as they interact on issues that are important to them. Several other children in the classroom also started to construct surveys on their own. Raphael's question, although he did not record it on his graph, was "Do your parents smoke?" (Figure 5–12). Crystal created another variation of Matt's initial idea: S NO TO SE (Say no to smoking) (Figure 5–13). She asked her classmates, "Do your parents

**Figure
5–11
Chris: "Does your daddy smoke?"**

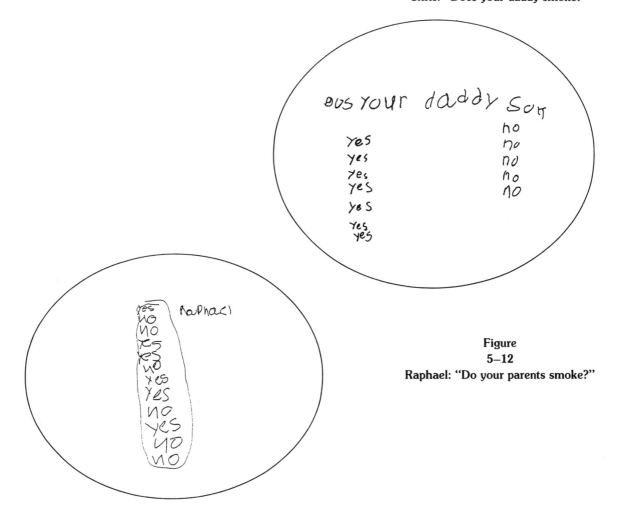

**Figure
5–12
Raphael: "Do your parents smoke?"**

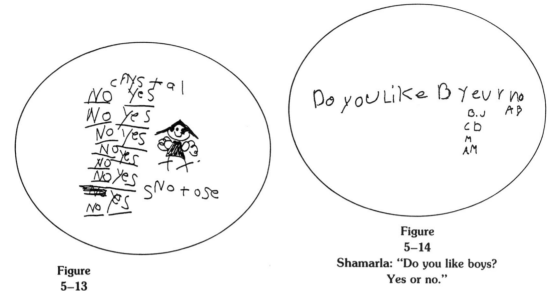

Figure
5–13
Crystal: "Say no to smoking."

Figure
5–14
Shamarla: "Do you like boys?
Yes or no."

smoke?'' Since her question was ambigious and did not refer specifically to mothers or fathers, she obtained some results that were different from Matt's and Chris's.

On this same morning Shamarla created a different survey: DO YOU LIKE B YEU R NO (Do you like boys? Yes or no) (Figure 5–14). She confided in the teacher that she was only asking girls this question because, of course, the boys would all say yes. Shamarla quite naturally and with no direct instruction used the technique of stratified sampling in her survey. Her method of using a subgroup for her sampling was quite reasonable. She demonstrated the ability to think strategically by recognizing the need to modify her survey to obtain the kind of information she desired. In this way Shamarla was learning about mathematics as she altered the typical process of gathering information in order to address her particular question. She felt free to explore a variation of the basic survey, showing her growing understanding that there are many options available for learners to gather and interpret information.

At class discussion time, Matt shared the results of his survey. After reading his question to the class he held his paper close to his chest while he counted his "yes" and "no" responses. Tim wrote Matt's survey question on the board, and columns for "yes" and "no." Matt counted five "yes" answers and eight "no" answers, and these were recorded on the board. When it was Chris's turn to describe his results he explained that he had recorded his answers in separate columns. His results were also written on the board. According to Chris's survey, seven fathers smoked and five fathers did not.

Matt: Does your mom smoke cigarettes?		*Chris:* Does your daddy smoke?	
Yes	No	Yes	No
5	8	7	5

Chris's efficient recording strategy of documenting "yes" and "no" answers in separate columns became obvious to everyone. While Matt had to count his answers individually to identify patterns in the data, Chris could see at a glance which response was greater by comparing the length of the two columns. By having the children share their formatting decisions Tim was allowing them to expand their knowledge of the potential variations for organizing numerical information. The children were learning through mathematics procedures for creating efficient and organized schemes for recording their data. As they discussed both surveys, the children continued to learn through graphing. "What can we tell by looking at these two?" Tim asked. Crystal's immediate response as she compared the "no" columns was "More mommies say no to smoking." "Matt gots more," said Chris, adding the number of respondents. "More daddies smoke," observed Shamarla. Her observation stemmed from a comparison of both graphs. She noticed that Matt found five mommies who smoked and Chris recorded seven daddies who did. Because Chris went beyond Matt's original idea by posing a question of his own the class discussion became richer and deeper. Chris's additional information provided the class with two sets of data, thereby increasing the opportunities for interpretation and analysis. The complementary nature of the information that these two young social scientists gathered and shared gave everyone a clearer picture of the smoking issue. They were true collaborators on a research topic of mutual interest.

Survey activities foster strategic thinking. Matt used what he knew about graphs and surveys to answer a question that was important and meaningful to him. Tim encouraged the children to generate variations on Matt's original question and to record their data in different ways. They shared their strategies and interpretations with each other. Because Tim showed respect for them as problem solvers and decision makers, they were willing to take risks, build on each other's ideas, and grow as literacy learners.

WHICH ONE DO YOU THINK RUNS THE FASTEST?

As soon as Jermaine arrived in the classroom one morning, Tim handed him a marker.

"Ask the class a question for our graph today," said Tim. Jermaine took the marker, paused, and thought for a few seconds.

"I don't know what to ask them," he replied.

"It can be anything you want," Tim reassured him. "You decide what you want to find out."

Jermaine stood by the large sheet of paper that Tim had taped onto the wall for him. After several minutes of thought he announced his plan: "I'm going to ask them, 'Which one do you think runs the fastest?' and they can pick a rabbit or a horse" (Figure 5–15).

He then turned to begin his drawings of the two animals. He hesitated, and looked to Tim.

"Hey, how do you draw a horse?"

**Figure
5–15
Which one do you think
runs the fastest?**

"Does anyone here know how to draw a horse?" asked Tim of the other students who stood nearby. Several children eagerly raised their hands. Jermaine chose Amanda, the class expert on horses. She had been drawing horses since the first day of school, and she incorporated them into almost every activity she pursued. Thus, Jermaine was learning to use the expertise of his peers to complete the task he had set for himself. Little did he know that Amanda would teach him some facts about horses in the process. After she completed her drawing Jermaine looked a bit puzzled.

"Hey, what about the tail?" he asked.

"It's a Tennessee walking horse—no, I mean a Clydesdale," remarked Amanda, in a somewhat authoritarian voice. To demonstrate what she meant, she began to simulate the movements of a Clydesdale. She clenched her fists, stiffened her arms, and pranced about the room in the typical gait of a Clydesdale, making a clomping noise with her mouth. Jermaine was learning through mathematics some additional information about the gait and appearance of a Clydesdale. Amanda's drawing of the Clydesdale's tail and her acting out its characteristic gait provided Jermaine with additional knowledge. When provided with opportunities to use each other as resources, children extend and refine each other's understanding.

When children are given ownership of a graph, they will pose questions that are meaningful for them. Jermaine was especially competitive in all his social endeavors, and his question reflected that competitive spirit. However, his idea was unique because no one in the room really knew the answer to the question, including Jermaine. This kind of question enhanced the children's understanding of the communicative potential of graphs. They noted that sometimes questions can be posed that have no definitive answer. The intent of this graph was to learn about people's preferences; the real answer could not be determined without further investigations. Adults are confronted with similar kinds of surveys, such as "Do you think life exists on Mars?", which seek opinions on questions that have as yet no answers.

Crystal was one of the first people to view Jermaine's graph. Before she signed her name beneath a choice, Jermaine read his question to her. Since he had assumed full responsibility for the graph by posing the question, directing the drawings, and creating the format, he wanted to be certain that the children were informed voters. He had noted in the past that some children merely signed under the choice that had the most names without bothering to read the question. Jermaine wanted to be sure that his graph reflected the true sentiments of the class. This kind of social learning is fostered when children are encouraged to engage in authentic mathematical experiences.

During the class discussion of Jermaine's graph several children wanted to find the real answer to the question. Raymond suggested calling a "farm man," while others mentioned several books in the room. The children were growing as strategic thinkers as they began to identify the potential resources available for solving their own problems. Other students wanted to explain the reasoning behind their vote. Ricky felt the rabbit would win and gave this justification: "The rabbit could go underground and the horse wouldn't know it, and then he would come up in front of him." These class discussions let the children explain their thinking in more detail and justify their decisions. The graph alone was limited in the kind of information it could convey.

As Jermaine tallied the results for his classmates, he was demonstrating the content knowledge he had gained through his survey. "It's eleven, y'all," he announced, pointing to the column for rabbits, "and five on that side. This one [the rabbits] has more."

"How many more?" Tim asked.

"Six," he promptly replied.

"How did you figure that out?" This question caused Jermaine to reflect on the process of his mathematical thinking. Jermaine's explanation showed how he learned about the mathematics system.

"I did it in my head," he explained. "See, five and five is ten, so I knew five and six—that's one more—is eleven." Another context for subtraction is a comparison situation, and graphs help to demonstrate this situation in a natural way. Jermaine used an adding-on strategy to solve his problem, figuring what addend was needed to increase five to the sum of eleven. His thinking demonstrated what a flexible problem solver he was. He related the problem to a fact that he already knew, that $5 + 5 = 10$. He then reasoned that by increasing one of the addends from five to six, he would change the sum from ten to eleven.

Mathematics is the study of relationships, not isolated facts.

Graphs provide a natural context for children to observe and use numbers in interesting relationships. Children are able to commit these basic facts to memory only when they have ample opportunities to use addition and subtraction in various contexts and to note relationships between numbers. Graphs provide a rich opportunity for promoting true understanding of such mathematical concepts.

Constructing Graphs to Make Classroom Decisions

WHAT COLOR SHOULD WE USE TO PAINT
THE PUPPET THEATER?

In the fall, Crystal brought two raggedy puppets to class. During her free-choice time that day Crystal and her friends played with the puppets constantly. They sang songs, told jokes and stories, and conversed via the puppets. Noting the enthusiasm for these puppets, Tim borrowed four additional puppets from the kindergarten class and made puppets one of the options during free-choice time. They were left out in a box in the book area for children to use with their friends. It was not long before the children were giving spontaneous puppet shows, using chairs for their stage.

The popularity of the puppet shows convinced Tim of the need for a permanent structure to house these performances. He brought to class a large, empty cardboard box and asked the children to suggest ways they could transform it into a puppet theater. They decided to cut a door in the back and a hole in the front for the stage. The children also thought it should be painted. Soon it became clear that no consensus could be reached about the color and that a decision would have to be made based on what the majority wanted. By this time the children already knew that graphs and surveys were a fair, if not perfect, way to decide matters involving group decisions. A large four-column graph was made with the question "What color should we use to paint the puppet theater?" Children suggested the color options, and during journal time they were encouraged to cast their vote. After the first few children had signed, it was obvious that blue was the most popular color (Figure 5–16).

While interpreting the graph at the class meeting, Katie suggested, with a degree of self-importance, that lots of children picked blue because "they knew it was going to win." The issue of winning had arisen many times during group discussions. To discourage the competitive aspect of graphs, Tim used terms like "most popular," "preferred," or "the item with the most choices."

**Figure
5–16
What color should we use
to paint
the puppet theater?**

The following week blue paint and brushes were made available to the children at recess and they transformed the large brown box into a puppet theater (Figure 5–17). The children were asked to sign the theater if they had participated in the process of creating it. Many drew pictures as well. Thus, they were gaining a deeper understanding of the purposes of graphs by using them as a vehicle for making an important classroom decision.

WHAT SHOULD WE NAME THE TURTLE?

Several years ago Tim rescued a small box turtle from the jaws of a dog. Shortly thereafter the turtle became his classroom

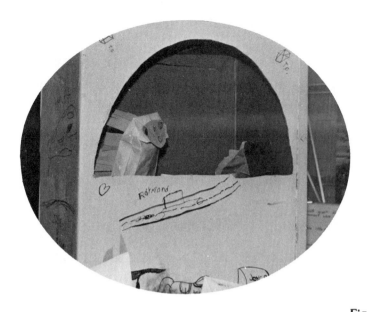

Figure
5–17
The puppet theater

pet. It was originally named Thomas by his second-grade class. This year during their study of animals, it became clear through descriptions of box turtles in books that Thomas was a female. A name change was in order.

It was decided that five names would be a good number from which to choose. The children were invited to suggest possible girl's names for the turtle. Immediately several hands went up. "Jenny," suggested Crystal. "That's my cousin's name." April offered the name Angela because it was her mother's name. Janice was the third name suggested. As James was called upon, he paused for a moment, looking around the room. Seeing the alphabet cards above the chalkboard, he focused on the Qq card, which had a picture of a queen on it. "I know, Princess!" he said. "That's my dog's name!" said Raphael emphatically. The fifth suggestion for a name was Lisa. The children were asked to think seriously about their choice, since they were assigning the turtle a name for the rest of her life. Each person was given a small slip of paper to record their vote. Most children kept their votes a carefully guarded secret. None of the votes was posted until everyone had had a chance to record a choice. The papers were then glued to the larger sheet of paper. Some children drew pictures, wrote the name they were voting for, and signed their papers; others simply wrote their favorite name (Figure 5–18).

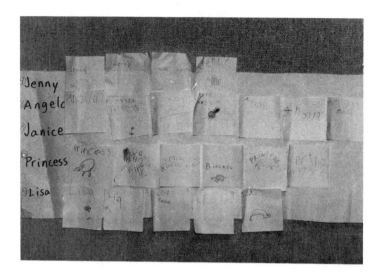

Figure
5–18
What should we name
the turtle?

WHAT TREAT WOULD YOU LIKE FOR THE FRIDAY PARTY?

On Friday afternoons the class often organized a small party, which consisted of a snack, often prepared by the children, and a game or outdoor recess. Several times during the school year the children chose the treats and activities for the party by using a graph. They always adhered to the decisions that were made.

One Wednesday a graph was taped on the wall for the children to sign as they came in. "What treat would you like for the Friday party?" was clearly written at the top. From the context and pictures, everyone could read the graph and knew how to respond (Figure 5–19).

April was the first person to sign the graph. She then took it upon herself to round up those who had not yet signed. She also tried to influence her classmates to vote for popcorn as she did. In order to convince her classmates that popcorn was the most popular choice, April wrote her name, her initials, her brother's name, and her sister's name all in one box. While not abandoning the convention of one box per person, she made the popcorn column appear to be more strongly supported. It was not just April, but her whole family, that enjoyed popcorn! April used the initials of her family members to expand the sign potential of her favorite choice. She knew that there was strength in numbers. If she could not convince others to vote for popcorn, perhaps her family could. Her strategy demonstrated another instance of learning through mathematics. She cleverly extended the meaning potential of her vote, while still following the restrictions of voting only once and keeping her signature confined to one box. April was refining her procedural knowledge of how graphs can be represented.

Chris, not to be swayed by April's subtle pressure, said, "I like peanuts more," and wrote his initials, C. L. J. The predominant use of initials on this graph followed a group discussion on punctuation, particularly how it was used for certain names. The discussion centered partly around B. J.'s name and how she always used two letters with periods to represent her first and middle names, Bonnie Jean. Chris, April, Ernie, Jason, Katie, Jermaine, Shamarla, and of course B.J. all used initials when signing this graph. Here the children were learning about written language by focusing on this particular feature of it.

When Rashaun signed his name, Shamarla, who was next in line, said in her best teacher's voice, "Rashaun, you can write your name better than that!" Rashaun obligingly rewrote his name much more conventionally over his first attempt. Children will often monitor each other's efforts when they are supported in an environment that encourages sharing and mutual respect.

During the interpretation of the graph, counting the exact total for each choice was not necessary because the result was obvious. The class noticed that Joyce had signed twice in the middle column. When Tim asked why this response was not appropriate, many clamored "It's unfair." "Why is that unfair," asked Tim, "when April and Rashaun also signed more than once?" Ricky looked at these multiple signatures and finally reasoned, "Because she used more than one box." Here again the children were learning through graphs by developing a sensitivity to the appropriate and inappropriate modifications of them. The experience also helped to demonstrate how graphs could be used as a medium to make decisions for classroom planning. The children were gaining an increased awareness of the expanding functionality and purposes of graphs in the daily life of their classroom.

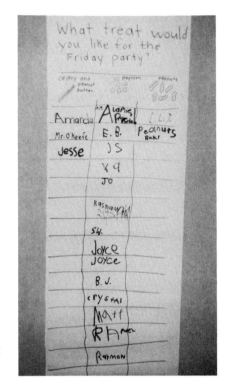

**Figure
5–19
What treat would you like
for the Friday party?**

Using Graphs to Learn

DO YOU LIKE TO HANDLE WORMS?

Another example of children using graphs to learn occurred during their study of animals. Tim had brought to school several worms to feed the classroom turtle. The children watched intently as the turtle enjoyed her imported dinner. Afterwards, some children, who had asked to hold the remaining worms, were allowed to do so. The next day Tim asked the children to respond to the question he had posed on the class graph: "Do you like to handle worms?" Those who said "no" could be heard mumbling their reasons to fellow classmates: "They're too slimey," "Yeah, they're too cold," "I don't like them because they're wet!" (Figure 5–20).

**Figure
5–20
Do you like to handle worms?**

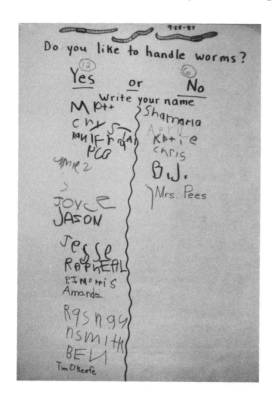

After everyone had signed the graph James walked by and studied it. He then turned to Tim and said, "All the girls don't like worms." He smiled quite smugly, glad that he was among the set of people who dared to say "yes" to worm holding!

"Are they all girls?" Tim asked.

"Let me see," he said, as he moved his finger to the top of the column labeled "No." He then began to find names that he could recognize.

"Shamarla . . . April . . . B. J. . . . Who is this?" he asked, pointing to the name of Mrs. Pees, one of the adults working in the room.

"Who do you think?" responded Tim.

James paused for a moment, staring at the name. Then he scanned the room, found Mrs. Pees, and pointed in her direction exclaiming, "Oh, it's her!"

"And whose name is this?" Tim asked, pointing to another name on the list.

"Chris?" he responded in a tentative voice.

"That's a good guess. It could be Chris, but it's a girl's name. It says Katie."

James was using the graph here as a means of learning to read the names of his classmates. He was also extending the original intent of the graph by proposing his own hypothesis, that only girls do not like to handle worms. As he began to read the list of names, he sought to confirm his prediction. The open-ended nature of this graphing experience provided James with the opportunity to pose his own hypothesis. One graph can often generate further questions, especially when children are given regular opportunities to discuss and interpret their findings. Thus through graphing James was learning to read the names of his friends by testing his own hypothesis about the data that were collected.

WHICH PINOCCHIO DO YOU PREFER?

In the midst of a literature unit on Pinocchio, Tim decided to use graphing to record the children's responses to three different versions of this classic. The class had recently finished reading and discussing the Collodi, Hillert, and Disney versions of Pinocchio. Tim had reproduced the cover of each on the graph. Knowing how sensitive the children were to illustrations, Tim was confident that they would be able to distinguish the books by their covers. Next, the books were placed under their rightful columns on the graph. During the class meeting Tim reminded the children about their recent investigation into the way different authors write. They used Pinocchio as a frame for the discussion. They looked again through each version of

**Figure
5–21**
Which Pinocchio do you prefer?

the story, reflecting on the author's style (Figure 5–21).

The children were then asked to document their preference. Raymond liked Disney's version and wrote "He is dancing in the puppet show." His illustration boasted a dancing puppet with wooden joints, sporting a fancy hat (Figure 5–22).

Jesse's dramatic illustration of a whale lunging out of the sea

**Figure
5–22**
**Raymond: "He is dancing
in the puppet show."**

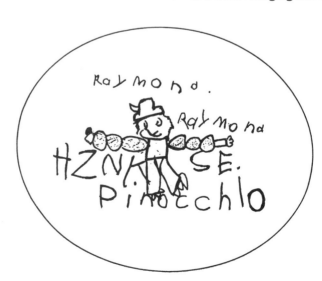

toward a small boat also included a written description: "Killer whale ate the father." He enthusiastically adopted the dramatic style of Collodi as his favorite (Figure 5–23).

B. J. also selected the Collodi style but for happier reasons. She wrote, "I like when Pinocchio got out of the whale's mouth" (Figure 5–24).

Giving children the opportunity to write and draw about their choices extended the graphing potential. In traditional graphing situations, the children's thinking is often limited to a narrow range of responses; their chance in this situation to clarify, document, and defend their choices using alternative forms of communication helped them to learn about this expanded communication potential.

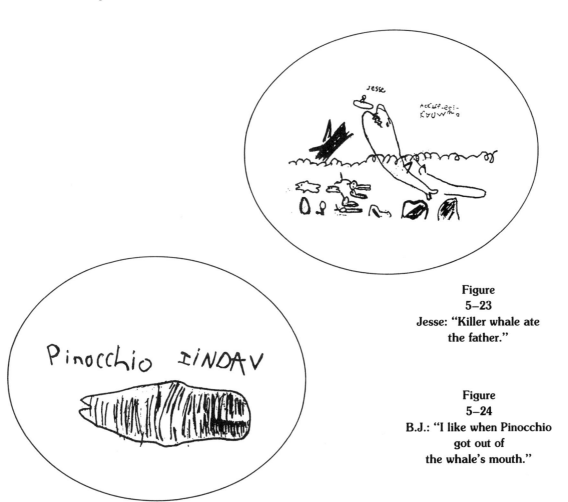

Figure
5–23
Jesse: "Killer whale ate
the father."

Figure
5–24
B.J.: "I like when Pinocchio
got out of
the whale's mouth."

While the children were putting the finishing touches on their papers, Tim suggested that two to three children at a time paste their responses on the graph. He was immediately surprised by Disney's poor showing. He was equally surprised to see how well the Hillert version of Pinocchio fared. He noted that the children who selected Hillert seemed to do so because of the illustrations. The children loved the artistic features of the text. Some children chose the Collodi version because they liked the detailed plot, characters, descriptive language, collage-like pictures, and many different subplots. The rich nature of this text had captured their attention.

When the children came together for discussion, their observations highlighted the potential for learning through graphs. "That one has eleven, it has the most!" exclaimed Jason. Shamarla was called on next. "One has eleven, the other one has four, and Disney only has one." Tim invited her to write the total for each column on the graph. Before doing so Shamarla led the class as they counted together the choices in each section. Next, Tim posed the question "How many more people liked Collodi than Disney?" Some children began using their fingers to solve this problem while others, like Jermaine, had an immediate response. He answered "Ten" and then explained his reasoning. "It's just like eleven take away one because only one person voted for Disney." Tim then posed similar questions using different choices. "How many more children liked Collodi than Hillert?" To capitalize on Jermaine's strategy and to encourage the children to teach each other how to solve problems, Tim invited Jermaine to explain how he would solve it. "See, you take away four from eleven and that makes seven." Tim wrote $11 - 4 = 7$ and then extended Jermaine's explanation by using the graph to show his thinking in a concrete way.

"The two columns are the same up to here," he said, pointing to the height of four squares, "but there are seven extra votes in the Collodi column." The discussion helped children learn through graphing about the comparison situation for subtraction. This mathematical concept was meaningful for the children because it grew out of an interest and experience that was relevant to their lives.

Katie raised her hand next to tell her classmates why she voted for Collodi. "When he made him, his nose got longer and longer." Her comment shifted the discussion from reading the graph mathematically to considering the meaning behind the children's preferences. The children began reading the choices. They compared different descriptions of specific events and characters, such as the ploy the fox and cat used to trick Pinocchio out of his money. They talked about how each author handled this event. April said that Collodi's version sounded as if it had really happened. Jesse told Tim to get the books so they could look at the pictures again. James noted a similarity: "They all have feathers in Pinocchio's hat."

The children's explanations show that readers construct different meanings when they read stories. These children made a variety of insightful observations concerning the characters, illustrations, and descriptive language of each story. What might traditionally be considered merely a mathematical activity evolved into a rich learning experience that helped Tim and the children learn through graphing more about addition, subtraction, and children's literature.

Summary

The use of graphs played an important role in the life of this classroom. Graphs were not viewed as an end in themselves, but as a tool for learning. As the children used them to answer meaningful questions about their world and to make informed decisions, they also expanded and refined their knowledge of the communication potential of graphs in various ways. The children were learning graphs, learning about graphs, and learning through graphs.

As the children created their own class graphs and personal surveys they demonstrated numerous insights about graphs. Chris helped them see that there was a more efficient way to record "yes" and "no" responses. Shamarla introduced the idea of stratified sampling by altering the set of people she chose to interview. Matt showed that graphs were limited in the kind of information they could convey; in his survey the degree of expertise in bicycle maintenance was not visible. Chris displayed the generative nature of personal surveys by extending Matt's initial question about smoking. As the children cast votes for a favorite version of Pinocchio they learned how art and language expanded the communication potential of their choice.

The children were also learning through graphs by increasing and refining their content and procedural knowledge. They had learned about the sex differences in turtles as they cast votes to rename the class pet. They had gained a deeper appreciation for children's literature as they voted for their favorite version of Pinocchio. The availability of graphs also empowered them as literacy learners because the graphs added to their knowledge of procedural options. The children now had more choices about how they could make decisions, solve problems, pose questions, and display information. In these ways they were learning more about the purposes, processes, and content of graphs. The experiences they had enabled them to broaden their understanding and refine their strategies as they continued to grow as learners of mathematics.

Personal Reflection

We knew that graphs had the potential to be a rich tool for learning, but we were amazed at the extent of that potential. We were fascinated by the children's growing skepticism of numerical information. They frequently questioned how the information was collected and whether it reflected the true sentiments of the class. They helped us gain a deeper understanding of the possibilities and limitations of graphical data by noting how surveys do not always reflect the feelings of respondents because of the way they pose their questions or define the categories of responses. We were also impressed with how children quite naturally incorporated these surveys and graphs into current themes of study, such as dinosaurs and health. We were learning that graphs, time lines, and other mathematical tools need to be made available so that the children have the opportunity to integrate them into different areas of study.

The insights we gained from the children's work with graphs and surveys caused us to ask ourselves further questions. Our new questions reflect our growing interest in discovering more about the learning potential of graphs for children when they are challenged to find new ways to display quantitative information:

1. What are other ways children can represent numerical information?
2. If we shared graphs and surveys from newspapers and magazines more often, how would children use these demon-

strations in their own work? We had shared a few surveys from *USA Today* at the beginning of the year but then stopped. If children were made aware of the diversity of graphs (such as the wide variety of topic choices as well as the variation in organization and format), they might incorporate some of these aspects into their own work.

3. What kind of learning would occur if children were challenged to represent the same data in different ways? Just as children are encouraged to revise written language to convey their intended feelings and descriptions, so too must they be challenged in mathematics to create alternative ways to display quantitative information. We saw this question as one possible way to discuss revision in mathematics learning.

4. How can graphs be used to introduce content knowledge? For instance, when Jermaine constructed his graph about rabbits and horses, we could have extended his question by investigating the speeds of various animals.

The children were helping us see the many ways they could use graphs as a vehicle for sharing and extending mathematical ideas.

6
VALUING CHILDREN'S MATHEMATICAL STRATEGIES

Only those who have
respect for the opinions of others
can be of real use to them.

Albert Schweitzer, in Edith Biggs and Robert McClean
Freedom to Learn

The importance of problem solving has been a dominant theme in the field of mathematics during the 1980s. In its *Agenda for Action* (1980), the National Council of Teachers of Mathematics urged that problem solving be the foundation of mathematics instruction. In its *Curriculum and Evaluation Standards for School Mathematics* (1989) the Council continues to emphasize the importance of this concern. Numerous problem-solving strategies have been identified and included in the instructional sequence of almost all mathematics textbooks. Such strategies include finding a pattern, making an organized list or chart, creating a drawing, acting out the problem, or simplifying the problem. These are helpful strategies, to be sure, but the crux of the matter is not the identification and transmission of strategies from teacher to pupil but rather an examination of how children come to know these strategies as they engage in purposeful mathematical enterprises. The emphasis must be shifted from teaching to learning, from instruction to demonstration. It is important that there be regular opportunities in classrooms for children themselves to share their own problem-solving strategies. As they do so, they view themselves as persons with unique insights and ideas and, as a result, continue to grow in their feelings of self-worth. Respect for children as competent problem solvers builds a climate of trust and mutual support. It pervades the atmosphere of a classroom and says to children, "I care about what you think and how you solve problems."

This care was demonstrated at a morning meeting of Tim's class as the children gathered on the rug to share some of their fingerprint stories. They had been investigating the different categories of fingerprint types and were now using their own fingerprints to write stories. Matt gave his story first (Figure 6–1). He pointed to the two arrows that he had drawn in the water and explained, "These are the two swans that went away." Jermaine studied Matt's drawing and responded in an astonished voice, "Hey, I never even thought of that!"

By encouraging Matt to make explicit his strategy for representing subtraction, Tim was not only validating his problem-solving effort but was also demonstrating for his classmates how they could use art to communicate mathematical ideas. Matt used an arrow, one of the earliest known symbols for subtraction, to convey the movement inherent in a take-away situation.

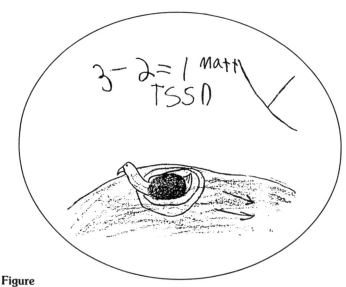

**Figure
6–1**
Matt: "There was three.
Then two went away.
There was one."

It is essential that children be given opportunities to tell their learning strategies. When children are provided with open-ended tasks that encourage them to solve problems in different ways, they inevitably create a host of problem-solving strategies that they are eager to share. If children are given time to explain their thinking and are respected as competent problem solvers, they will not hesitate to share what they know. In fact, children ought to be supported as educational researchers in their own right (Brown 1974). By valuing children's strategies, we encourage them to devise and compare efficient methods for solving a variety of problems.

Mathematical Concepts and Strategies for Understanding

Throughout this book we have demonstrated how children devised unique strategies for understanding mathematical concepts. In the case of graphs, for example, we predicted some of the strategies they would use, such as using graphs to understand better the comparison and missing-addend situations for subtraction. However, most of their strategies we did not foresee, and it was through the childrens' sharing of these strategies that we grew as learners. For instance, we knew that graphs provided an interesting vehicle for exploring mathematical understanding, particularly since they are multimodal affairs involving reading, writing, drawing, conversing, and counting. However, the diversity and complexity of the childrens' strategies caused us to reflect on our own understanding of graphs. The children helped us see in a new way the rich potential for learning that is inherent in statistical investigations. A summary of their strategies is given below:

Mathematical Concepts	*Strategies for Understanding*
Understanding statistics	Noticed that the use of size of responses can be misleading
	Devised unique recording systems to differentiate responses
	Created visual representations that were appropriate for the question asked
	Used stratified sampling to poll only a selected group of people
	Questioned the validity of numerical information
	Used art and language to expand the communication potential of their choice
	Analyzed certain surveys to discover they were limited in the kind of information they could convey
	Used graphs to expand their knowledge of current themes of study and personal interests

Many of the strategies that the children devised were connected to classroom themes of study. During the dinosaur study unit, for example, the children addressed concepts that involved an understanding of measurement, time, and classification.

Mathematical Concepts	Strategies for Understanding
Understanding measurement	Used yardsticks and rulers to make comparisons of dinosaurs in the hallway and on the playground
Understanding time	Used time lines to compare the age of dinosaurs with other historical events
Understanding classification	Classified dinosaurs according to a variety of attributes, such as size, diet, strength, and method of defense

Children created other strategies as they were invited to tell stories about raising fish or losing and growing teeth.

Mathematical Concepts	Strategies for Understanding
Understanding story problems	Devised stories that included multiple events
	Created stories with "extraneous" information
	Used the language of mathematics to write and tell their stories
	Revised story problems so that art, mathematics, and language worked together to tell the story
Understanding time	Used drawings and numbers to illustrate a series of events that occurred over time

Through writing stories, conducting surveys, and learning through group themes (dinosaurs) and personal themes (bicycles, smoking, babies), the children were also gaining a broader understanding of addition and subtraction.

Mathematical Concepts	Strategies for Understanding
Understanding addition and subtraction	Created dinosaur stories to show set-within-set situation for subtraction

Mathematical Concepts	Strategies for Understanding
Understanding addition and subtraction (*continued*)	Used distance model on board games to show addition and subtraction
	Used color, spacing, symbols (such as bubbles and *X*'s), and partial figures to represent addition and subtraction situations
	Used one or two drawings to show the inverse relationship between addition and subtraction
	Demonstrated various names for a number by classifying a set of dinosaurs in different ways
	Made observations about graphs that involved comparison and missing-addend situations of subtraction
	Used graphs to add total number of responses

In this chapter we would like to discuss some other strategies that the children used to understand the following concepts: zero, patterns, basic mathematical principles, and story problems. Most of the strategies the children devised grew out of stories they were writing; a few came from those using their fingers. Their strategies demonstrate how they chose to highlight a specific aspect of their experience for learning mathematics, learning about mathematics, and learning through mathematics.

Understanding Zero

Understanding zero has often been a difficult concept for children. It is important that children come to understand that zero is not nothing; it does represent something! Children can develop this understanding if they are given opportunities to record the absence of things in different contexts. When children are engaged in open-ended experiences, they will draw upon their own background knowledge and interests to create contexts for zero that are meaningful for them.

April created a fish story in which she used the concept of zero. The class had not been very successful in raising fish. Several of the goldfish died and had to be replaced. April represented one of the healthier fish in her story by writing, "0 fish die" (Figure 6–2). She used zero to represent not the

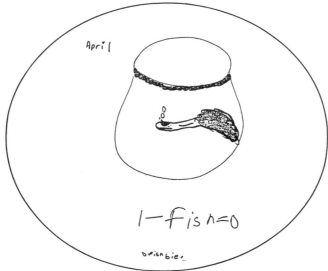

**Figure
6–2
April: "0 fish die."**

death of the fish but its continued healthy existence in the tank. The bubbles rising from its head further reiterate its state of good health. In this way April used zero to placehold the action of continued healthful living.

Jesse's strategy for understanding zero also involved showing the results of a particular action (Figure 6–3). He pointed to the 0 above the empty mouth and said, "Zero means no teeth." Then, pointing to the larger 0 at the bottom of the page, he explained, "If they don't see the little one they can see the big one!" Jesse understood that the size of a zero did not affect its meaning. His two drawings nicely conveyed the notion that life did exist before zero. His top drawing showed that Jimmy did in fact possess eight teeth before the accident. The bottom drawing, which Jesse labeled with a 0, indicated the results of

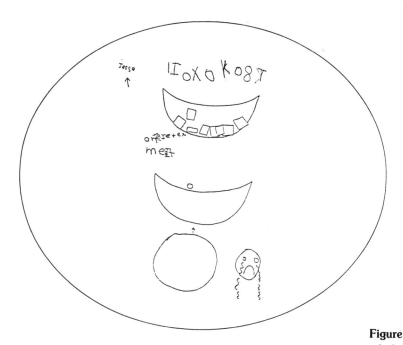

**Figure
6–3**
**Jesse: "One time there was
a boy named Jimmy.
He had eight teeth.
One time he was riding his bike
and cracked
all of his teeth."**

the accident. Here again zero represented something: a lack of teeth. The two drawings allow the reader a glimpse of the total context for zero by showing what Jimmy's mouth was like before and after the accident. Thus, zero placeholds a point in time, and a sad one at that. A different kind of life did exist for Jimmy before the accident!

James anticipated life after zero when he wrote and drew his own playground story (Figure 6–4). He placed ten small photographs of his classmates in a tree. He then drew an empty swing set and placed a partial photograph of those same swings on his paper. In this instance James used zero to tell the reader that there were no children on the swings right now but then used his written text to indicate that this condition would soon be changing: "Some people are going to go on the swing." Just as Jesse's two drawings helped the reader visualize what life was like before zero, James's strategy highlights a slightly different state of zero—a period of inactivity on the swings—which will change sometime in the future as children climb down from the tree and move on to another activity. These experiences provide children opportunities to learn about the mathematical system by allowing them to explore ways to use zero to placehold the ideas they wish to convey. As children

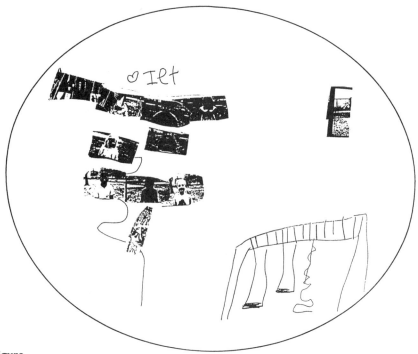

**Figure
6–4**
**James: "It's ten people
in the tree.
Some people are going
to go on the swing."**

share their strategies with each other they are also learning through mathematics by becoming aware of the increased number of procedural options available to them to communicate their observations of the world.

Raymond also created a playground story but used a somewhat different strategy for understanding zero (Figure 6–5). As he explained his story further he said, "One person going up and one person going down, so 1 and 1 is 2." He interpreted his $2 - 4 = 0$ by saying, "I put a 2 right here because there's two on the slide, and then there's two on the monkey bars so that's four." He then pointed to the 4 in his equation. "And then I took away all of them, and then I have 0," he said, covering over all four photographs with his hands. Although his equation is not conventional, his explanation demonstrates his understanding of the process. Unlike James, who used zero to anticipate the activity that was to come, Raymond employed zero to show an activity that had already occured. Both were exploring the processes of the mathematical sign system and were learning how it could be used to represent slightly different situations.

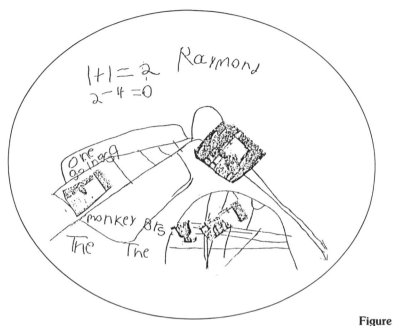

**Figure
6–5**
**Raymond: "One is going up
the monkey bars.
1 + 1 = 2.
2 − 4 = 0."**

Sometimes children explore the affective dimension of zero. April drew a picture of a girl crying as she sat beside two colorful birds. She wrote "$2 - 2 = 0$" and then explained her story further: "The girl was crying because her parrots died." In this way April explored the feeling of loneliness that can be associated with zero. Jesse also included this emotional dimension into his tooth story by drawing a weeping child. In both instances the children were expanding the meaning potential of zero.

Daehoon explored the meaning of zero further by trying to express a similar idea using written language. He had divided six presents between two people in various ways and used a number sentence to record his actions (Figure 6–6). In his last example he glued six presents under the first person and wrote the equation "$6 + 0 = 6$." He then looked at the blank space underneath the second person and felt something was missing. He wrote "No" there and explained his action by saying, "I put a 'no' right there because there are none." Thus, Daehoon was focusing on how mathematics, art, and written language worked to communicate the absence of presents.

Jesse made a subtle distinction in another kind of story. The children had been learning about Christmas traditions in dif-

**Figure
6–6
Daehoon's work**

ferent cultures. Jesse chose to focus on lights by gluing six
candles on each tree. He then wrote a 6 inside the first tree
and added beneath it, "This tree is light"; he drew a 0 inside
the second tree and wrote, "This tree is not light" (Figure
6–7). Jesse used zero to represent not the number of candles
but rather their qualitative state of being lit or not lit. His re-
finement of the particular attributes of candles gave zero a more
subtle meaning. Jesse too was learning through mathematics

**Figure
6–7
Jesse: "This tree is light.
This tree is not light."**

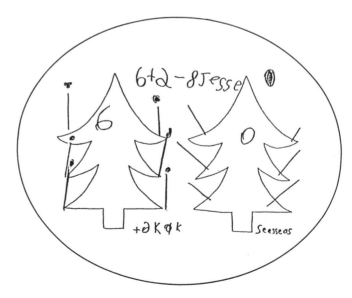

as he explored the fine distinctions that can be communicated through the use of zero.

Children come to understand these distinctions for zero when they have regular opportunities to construct them for themselves. They must use mathematics for real purposes. The complexity of events that surrounds number use is crucial to supporting an understanding of the functionality of numbers. Textbooks would not dare expose children to the complex range of meanings of zero that these children explored. In fact, textbooks have responded in quite the opposite way by simplifying problems, thereby removing numbers from a meaningful context. However, children show themselves to be competent problem solvers when they are given ownership of real problems connected to their life.

Understanding Patterns

Humans come equipped with ready-made counters. Children often use their fingers (and sometimes their toes) to solve problems and uncover insights about mathematical patterns. It is a sad irony, however, that in some classrooms children are forbidden to use their fingers even though a brief glimpse at the history of mathematics reveals a long line of numeration systems from various cultures that are organized around base ten (fingers) or base twenty (fingers and toes). In fact, most adults still use their fingers to perform counting in certain situations; for example, how many more months until my child's birthday, or at what time do I have to go back outside and put more money in the parking meter? The important point here is that fingers are an accessible and valuable tool for counting, and children can use them to highlight significant mathematical patterns.

Shamarla used her fingers to discover one such interesting pattern. She wrote $1 + 4 = 5$ on her paper to describe the playground story she had created in which one person was on the monkey bars and four other children were playing on the swings. She looked at what she had written and decided to make another equation using some of the same numbers. She wrote $5 + 4 = 9$. This second equation was not related to any particular event in her story; instead, it grew out of her decision to convey this particular aspect of the mathematics system.

"How did you figure out that five and four is nine?" asked Tim. This question focused Shamarla's attention on how the mathematics system worked.

"See, five and five is ten," she replied, holding up all her fingers, "and then take one down and it's nine." Shamarla used her fingers to demonstrate her creative thinking strategy; she cleverly used a doubles fact, $5 + 5 = 10$, to help her learn another closely related fact. Shamarla was coming to realize that mathematics is not the study of isolated number facts but rather a system concerned with the relationships between those facts.

Shamarla continued her explanation by uncovering further patterns: "So five and four is nine, and if you put another finger down, that's eight—five and three; and another one down is seven—five and two; then six, five, four, three, two, one, zero." She acted out this descending pattern with her fingers as she described each step. Again Shamarla was noting the relational aspect of number facts by using the sub-base of five to rename the upper decade numbers, such as $6 = 5 + 1$, $7 = 5 + 2$, $8 = 5 + 3$, $9 = 5 + 4$, and $10 = 5 + 5$. The Romans had a sub-base of five in their numeration system. Their symbol for 5 was V, which is said to represent the gap between the thumb and pointer of an outstretched hand. Their symbol for 10, X, is said to represent two sets of 5. Like the Romans, Shamarla was using her fingers to show the connection between the number facts greater than 5 and those less than 5. She was learning about mathematics as she came to view this system as an organizational scheme replete with unique patterns and relationships.

Veronica uncovered still another interesting mathematical pattern by using her fingers. A few days earlier Tim had to count the number of people who had returned their homework assignment. He looked at the class chart and counted by twos, "Two, four, six, eight, ten."

"What are you doing?" asked Quinton.

"I'm counting by twos," said Tim. He explained how he grouped the children by twos and skip-counted by sets of two instead of having to count each one separately.

Veronica was intrigued by this method of counting. She had already had a lot of experience counting by ones and twos as she jumped rope outside on the playground. Now, as she waited in line to go to lunch, she used her ready and accessible fingers to demonstrate this counting pattern in a new way.

"Hey, Mr. O'Keefe, look," she said. She held up only the pointers on both hands and said "Two." Then she held up both middle fingers and said "Four"; she continued to raise one finger on each hand until she reached ten. Her strategy nicely demonstrated the evenness of skip counting by showing the numerical symmetry of each even number; it also pointed out an interesting number pattern inherent in the double facts: $1 + 1 = 2, 2 + 2 = 4, 3 + 3 = 6, 4 + 4 = 8,$ $5 + 5 = 10$. As Veronica explained her strategy at a class meeting her classmates acted out this pattern by using their own fingers. At one point Brandon remarked, "Hey, I think I can count by twos in another way, like one, three, five, seven, nine." His insight led the other children to use their fingers to explore this pattern. Thus, the children were learning that there were at least two ways to count by twos. Such a discovery is not always obvious. For instance, children often consider that the only way to count by tens is ten, twenty, thirty, forty, fifty, and so on. When they are asked to count by tens starting at seventeen, a common reply is "You can't do that!" Veronica's revelation about skip counting by using her fingers helped to initiate this fruitful discussion of the different ways of counting.

Understanding Basic Mathematical Principles

Children also use this strategy of finger reckoning to understand better some basic mathematical principles. Daehoon used his fingers to uncover the mathematical principle of compensation. He was using two colors of blocks to show names for four. He held up one finger on one hand and three fingers on the other hand to show the combination of blocks that he had made. He stared at his fingers for a moment, and then raised one finger on his first hand and lowered one finger on his other hand.

"Hey, look, it's two and two," he observed. "Three and one is like two and two. They're four." He shared his insight with Tim several times and kept raising and lowering his fingers to demonstrate his finding. In his own way Daehoon had uncovered an interesting principle in mathematics known as the law of compensation: adding a value of one to one addend and subtracting the value of one from another addend do not affect the sum. More complex additions can be solved by applying this same principle:

$$49 + 33 = 50 + 32 = 82$$

or

$$198 + 241 = 200 + 239 = 439$$

Thus, by using his fingers Daehoon was able to explore mathematical processes and gain a unique insight into how the mathematics system works.

It was also Daehoon and several other children who noted the law of commutativity as they worked with certain materials and created their own mathematical stories. This law states that the order in which one combines addends does not change the sum. This is an extremely important relationship to discover, since it reduces the number of basic facts to be learned in addition by one half. Daehoon gained this insight by playing a number game with a set of beans. The beans were painted red on one side and left white on the other. He placed six beans in a small film can, shook it, and recorded the different combinations that appeared. Each time he recounted the beans as he placed them back in his cup. After recording his combinations for several times he noted that the sums were always six and he remarked, "Hey, they're all six. I know why they're all six, because they're six beans." His counting aloud and written repetition of six helped Daehoon see that there was stability to the number six despite the surface differences in color combinations. Later on he made another observation: "Hey, look, it goes back and forth—two and four, and four and two." Now knowing that the sum was always six, he noted this back-and-forth pattern of the addends. Daehoon was coming to understand the commutativity principle as he sought to describe it in his own way.

Other children discovered this same mathematical principle in slightly different contexts. Jermaine wrote a story using some of his fingerprints and then recorded some numbers to convey the events of his story: $1 + 1 = 2$. He particularly enjoyed trying to list all the names he could for a particular number. However, when he looked at this equation, he turned to Tim and said, "I don't have to do it the other way, it's just the same!" Jermaine realized that turning around a doubles combination would not change his sum. Although this insight is not always obvious to children, Jermaine helped to demonstrate this mathematical principle to his peers by focusing on this particular aspect of the mathematical system.

Ricky saw the commutativity principle in operation when he created a playground story (Figure 6–8). As he shared his story

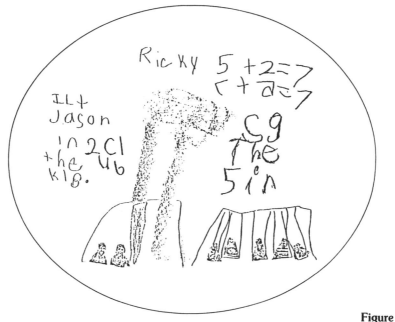

**Figure
6–8**
Ricky: "I let Jason in the club.
Two in the club.
Five on the swings.
5 + 2 = 7.
2 + 5 = 7."

he pointed to the two equations he had written at the top of his paper and remarked, "Both ways it equals seven." What is particularly interesting about Ricky's story is that his insightful observation about the system of mathematics is embedded in a rather complex story. There are children swinging as well as others who are negotiating permission to join a club. Traditional textbooks would not have included both of these events in a single story problem for fear that such extraneous events as club membership would only hinder a child's understanding. Not only was Ricky not confused by the complexity of the story but he was also challenged to discover an important mathematical principle. There were no distracting details from Ricky's perspective. Club membership was an important issue on the playground, and his inclusion of that detail made perfect sense to him.

Chris described his insight about the commutativity principle in another way. After he had discovered different Christmas present allocations for the number six, Tim noted his combinations of 2 + 4 and 4 + 2. Chris giggled and then replied, "Yeah, I know. I just turned them around." Chris found it humorous that even though the combinations were slightly different, the sum still remained the same. Humor is often an integral part of mathematical discoveries. Chris smiled because he enjoyed explaining this numerical trick—his representations (2 + 4 and 4 + 2) appeared on the surface to be different, but the total number of presents was not changed.

At other times during the year the children's discussions would sometimes focus on different ways for writing equations. Raphael, like Chris, recorded different combinations of six Christmas presents that must be divided between two people. For his first solution he glued three presents down beneath each person, wrote "6 3 3," and said, "Six presents. Three and three." Jermaine, always intent on the "right" way, overheard this remark and commented, "That ain't how you say it. It's three and three is six." "No," said Raphael, equally intent on justifying his own decision. "You can do it this way too. Six presents, three and three." The children were actively engaged in testing out their notions of how to represent a given mathematical experience. Each surface representation (6 = 3 + 3 and 3 + 3 = 6) was correct, but each conveyed a slightly different emphasis. Jermaine, who throughout the year was always concerned that everyone follow the classroom rules and be fair, wanted to emphasize the equal partitioning of the presents and sought to convey this fairness with the equation of 3 + 3 = 6. Raphael, on the other hand, chose to emphasize the total number of presents that were to be distributed and used the equation of 6 = 3 + 3 to note this particular aspect of the experience. The important point is not that these two children ever resolved the issue (each remained adamant throughout the discussion) but that the question arose. Children would encounter both forms of notation in mathematics textbooks. However, these conventional forms of representation make more sense to children if they have the opportunity to discuss and argue about them from their own personal experience. Children gain a deeper understanding of the conventions of the mathematics system if they can be active participants in exploring this system themselves. Raphael and Jermaine's discussion also highlighted the subtle changes of meaning conveyed by each equation. Children uncover these subtle distinctions when they investigate problems that they themselves have generated and have a vested interest in trying to communicate.

Understanding Story Problems

Mathematics, like language, is an open system that permits learners to explain and explore their world. It is not a static system that merely maintains meaning. Rather, in using mathematics, learners are supported in not only clarifying their thinking but also discovering new insights about the mathematical system. Many of these insights occur as children construct their own stories.

Katie demonstrated her own discovery about zero when she wrote a playground story. She read her story as: "There are these two swinging, and there could be two more [pointing to the empty swings], so two and two is four" (Figure 6–9).

**Figure
6–9**
**Katie: "There are these two swinging,
and there could be
two more,
so two and two is four."**

Katie's story has a certain level of abstractness about it since half of the people in her story are not represented. However, the empty swings placehold their presence. She was expanding the meaning potential of zero by explaining a hypothetical extension to her artistic representation—that even though at the moment there are zero people on the two empty swings, the swings could be occupied later. After discussing her first story with Tim, Katie created another interesting one: "And you can do this. If you take away this one [she pointed to the child on the swings], and put two right here [she pointed to the two empty swings], it would be three." Her second story was quite complex, involving two separate actions: one child leaving $(2 - 1 = 1)$, and then two other children joining the group $(1 + 2 = 3)$. Because she had repeated opportunities to return to her text, she was able to create another plausible story from her visual representation. Brown and Walter (1983) have termed this playfulness with certain variables in the story "the art of problem posing." As Katie shuffles around the persons in her story and creates another variation, she gains a deeper understanding of the diversity and the interrelatedness of story problems. The more opportunities learners have to change and modify story variables, the more willing they are to question story information and pose their own problem extensions. This playfulness and ingenuity free learners from the "right answer" syndrome and support them in their quest for generating problems, not just answering them (Brown and Walter 1983).

Jesse generated several mathematical stories after he glued down pictures of six dinosaurs (Figure 6–10). He began with the dinosaurs at the bottom of his page. He wrote below them

**Figure
6–10
Jesse's dinosaur story**

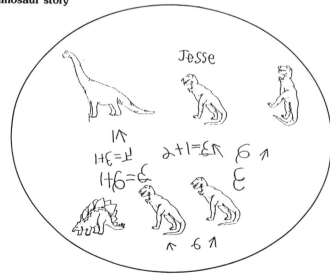

"1," "2," and then "1 + 2 = 3" in the space above them. Here he combined two different types of dinosaurs, using arrows to indicate which two were the same. He then wrote the equation "1 + 3 = 4" and drew "1" above it. Since addition is a binary operation (meaning that only two numbers can ever be added at one time), Jesse used the set of three dinosaurs at the bottom of the page for one group because this group had already been combined from his first equation. It was then combined with a different dinosaur from the top line to make a sum of four. The equation of 2 + 1 + 3, which he wrote as 2 + 1 = 3, combines the two sets of dinosaurs on the first line and then indicates the uniting of both sets of three to reach a total of six dinosaurs. Jesse's knowledge of dinosaurs contributed to the generative nature of this experience; his mathematical equations reflect a diverse set of classification schemes as he combined these animals according to their type as well as their placement on the page.

Jermaine also classified story figures. As part of their lengthy study of animals the children were encouraged to cut out and classify a large set of animals. Jermaine divided his paper in half and wrote: "Big. Little. Most of them is little" (Figure 6–11). He wrote 6 + 8 = 14. He then turned to Tim and said, "You could do it this way too," and he proceeded to write 8 + 6 = 14. However, even the recognition of the commutativity principle was not sufficient for Jermaine. He wanted to continue to explore different number combinations, and had made similar investigations during previous mathematical experiences. At this point he abandoned his original intent of classifying animals and decided to pursue the more interesting challenge of renaming fourteen in as many ways as he could. One of the driving forces behind learning is the learner's desire to explore new and interesting hypotheses rather than rehearse old ones (Harste, Woodward, and Burke 1984).

"There's other ways you can do it too," he explained and began to list other possible numerical sets for fourteen animals: 13 + 1, 12 + 2, 11 + 3, and so forth. As he recorded these names for fourteen, Jermaine made interesting insights about the mathematics system itself. After writing 8 + 6 = 14, Jermaine then wrote 7 + 5. He paused, looked at what he had written, and remarked, "Hey, that ain't right. Seven and five is twelve." He then erased his 5, recorded a 7, and wrote 7 + 7 = 14.

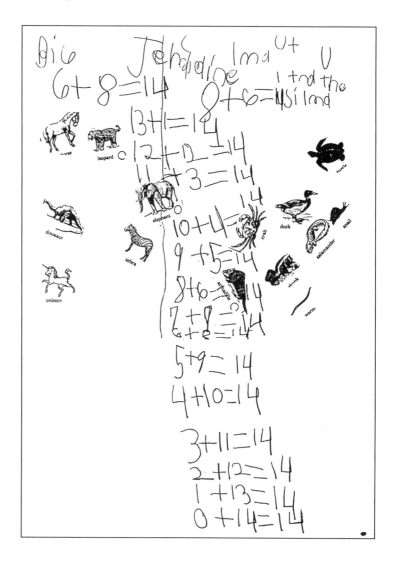

Figure
6–11
Jermaine: "Big. Little.
Most of them
is little."

"Why do you suppose you wrote a 5?" asked Tim.

"I thought it [the numerical sequence] went down but it went up," he explained. Jermaine realized there was a pattern to the solutions he was devising and predicted the column of second addends would decrease just as the first column had done. However, he encountered an anomaly when the sum did not equal fourteen. He focused his attention on the pattern again and realized that the first column reflected a descending order and the second column an ascending order. He confirmed this observation as he wrote 7 + 7 = 14, 6 + 8 = 14, pointed to the 7s and said, "Right here they tied"; he then pointed to the 8 and said, "Right here, this [the second column] is bigger now." Jermaine used the problem-solving strategy of finding a pattern with great flexibility; he used it to predict the number sequence that he was generating as well as to resolve the anomaly that he encountered. As he completed his pattern he made one final remark about his findings. He pointed to the equation $0 + 14 = 14$ and said, "This one [equation] looks like it wouldn't be much [pointing to the zero], but it is; see [pointing to the fourteen]." Jermaine was reflecting on the deceptive appearance of this particular equation. When zero is listed as the first of two addends, it would seem to indicate a small sum. However, if the second addend is quite large, the sum can still be substantial. Thus, by generating multiple classification schemes to represent fourteen animals, Jermaine also gained a broader understanding of the mathematics system.

Summary

When children are provided the time to share their mathematical strategies for solving problems, they demonstrate remarkable insights about how this system works (Figure 6–12). These children expanded the meaning potential for zero by using zero to indicate a state of healthful living, to express

**Figure
6–12
Aaron sharing strategies**

loneliness, or to anticipate events that were soon to occur. They used their fingers, the most convenient mathematical manipulative, to highlight other significant aspects of the mathematics system, such as the principle of compensation and the symmetry of even numbers. The children used their own language to describe the commutativity principle when they found it operating in various situations. Through class discussions they focused attention on different ways to record a given story numerically. Finally, the generative nature of the mathematics system enabled these children to tell various stories and to gain a deeper appreciation for the patterns that lie beneath the surface of so many mathematical investigations.

Personal Reflection

The creative strategies that these children devised caused us to think again how we could best support them as learners. We posed these questions for ourselves:

1. How can we help children be more reflexive about the strategies they are using? We thought that if the children were given other opportunities to make their strategies known, they would become more reflexive and would monitor these strategies more critically.
2. How can we support children in evaluating the appropriateness of their strategies in different contexts? For instance, how could Jesse use his strategy for classifying dinosaurs in other areas of study? How could Veronica use her counting strategy of twos to understand division situations?
3. What other mathematical principles could children uncover by using their fingers? We were fascinated by the strategies the children devised and were eager to know what other mathematical patterns they might discover.

7
CREATING A COMPREHENSIVE MATHEMATICS CURRICULUM

Wallowing in correctness,
being hell-bent for "mastery,"
stops learning.
Messes are the fodder of creativity.

Dorothy Watson, Carolyn Burke, and Jerome Harste
Whole Language: Inquiring Voices

Learning Naturally: When Parents Celebrate and Support Children's Mathematical Investigations

Twenty-one-month-old Zachary spent a great deal of time doing "business." As he worked, he naturally used language and mathematics to get his business done.

This young child took his enterprises very seriously. He approached his grandmother to acquire all of the necessary tools for "business" or "office." "Grammy, need checkbook." His grandmother complied by tearing out deposit slips. "Geen pen" was Zachary's next request. After gathering these resources, he took a calculator that was sitting on the edge of the dresser and made a desk from a suitcase on the floor. While the adults continued their conversation, he went to work.

"How many candies?" was his first inquiry.

His mother responded, "I think four would be good."

"Four, six, seven, eight" were his remarks as he pressed the calculator's buttons. Next, he took his green pen and wrote the transaction on the deposit slips. His marks may have looked random to outside observers, but his family knew exactly what they meant.

"Cookies, seven, nine, five, twee." Again, Zachary systematically recorded this transaction (Figure 7–1).

Figure 7–1
Zachary doing "business"

149

"Tim, twee cakes?" he asked before pressing the buttons on his number machine.

"That sounds good," Tim replied.

"OK, good, fine," he said, acknowledging Tim's order. "Twee, five, seven, nine."

Zachary approached every adult in the room. Each interaction was complete with numerical information that represented candies, cakes, and pizza orders. He approached his mother again.

"Momma, four candies, momma?"

His mother responded, "Sure, momma will take four candies and Hannah will have two."

Zachary talked his way through the transaction, "Momma, four candies." He pressed the numerals on the calculator, recorded the order in his "checkbook," and paused for a moment. He glanced back at his mother and asked, "Hannie like two?" His mother had begun conversing with his three-month-old sister and didn't hear his question. His sweet melodic voice became a bit more forceful as he put his little hands on his mother's cheeks and turned her face so that their eyes met. "You hear me?" he asked. "Do more business!"

"I'm sorry, Zach. I said momma would like four candies and Hannah will have two."

"OK, Hannie like two candies!" Zachary had already calculated his mother's order and so simply completed his sister's (Figure 7–2, A and B).

Insights from Parents

We were fascinated by Zachary's behavior. He was so serious about this business endeavor. We shared our educational insights with his parents. They listened for a few moments with puzzled looks on their faces. We thought that we might be using educational jargon that was unfamiliar to them and so attempted to explain our excitement again. They were not confused by our initial explanation; instead, they wondered why we did not know that kids do these things all the time. They intuitively appreciated Zachary's efforts and could also infer meaning from his strategies.

His mother explained his actions as follows:

When Zachary does business he goes from person to person.

A
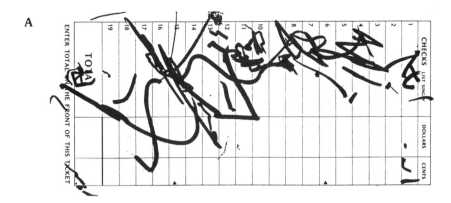

B
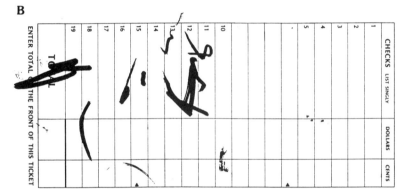

**Figure
7–2
Zachary's orders.
A: "Twee, five, seven, nine."
B: "Momma, four candies."**

He says similar things to each person. Sometimes the
sentences are questions and sometimes they are statements.
You can tell what he means by listening to his voice. He
always presses numbers on his calculator. He knows that
the numbers mean "how much" of something. While he
uses various numbers every time he takes an order and
he doesn't press the exact numbers he is saying, he knows
what the general process of doing business is all about. He
also differentiates between letters and numbers. He always
refers to numbers when using the calculator. He uses numbers
and writing in the same ways we do when we do business.
He is so serious too. It's like he is on a mission.

I know you might think I am imagining this but his writing
and drawing are different. When he writes on the deposit
slip he uses small lines. He lifts the pen off the paper and
makes several marks per order. He doesn't read his marks
to me because he doesn't need to. He knows that we know
what they mean. When he draws pictures, his pen never

A

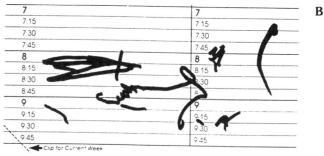

B

**Figure
7–3
Zachary's work.
A: Drawing.
B: Writing.**

leaves the paper. He makes big circular motions and goes all over the paper. He always wants to tell me about his drawings. You can see a difference in his drawing and writing, and he doesn't need to tell you about his business because it is already understood [Figure 7–3, A and B].

Oh, yeah, he even writes on business cards in a different way than he does on deposit slips. When writing on business cards he documents "'pointments." He looks at his father's old watch that he wears daily and says things like, "Want to see at four o'clock?" Then he writes down your response [Figure 7–4]. He also does this on appointment books. One day he was working in his appointment book and he looked up and asked, "No color on appointment book?" I told him

that he was right. We write appointments in our books. He
spoke under his breath, "Unhuh, no, unhuh."

Learning from Zachary and His Parents

Zachary was only twenty-one months old when he demonstrated sophisticated mathematical reasoning. While we marveled at his ingenious transactions and fondly reflected upon his "cute" expressions, Zachary caused us to consider what school-age children could do if provided with rich experiences and continuous support.

Although we learned a lot from Zachary's business transactions, we were also privileged to consider them in light of his parents' interpretation. It became very clear to us that the natural learning experiences that occurred daily in this family represented what we had been considering as a theoretical frame for curriculum. Zachary's parents provided continual demonstrations about how language and mathematics work to get things done, to record ideas and understandings, and to share these with others. They had naturally provided opportunities for Zachary to grow in mathematical literacy by demonstrating the uses of language, art, and mathematics. They allowed Zachary to engage in the same kinds of "work" that they did. He was allowed to use the same resources and received the same kind of meaningful feedback that they do when they work. In other words, he was respected as a thoughtful decision maker. They did not question his efforts. Instead, they read meaning into his behavior and understood that his actions were far from random. They naturally supported and extended his thinking by creating new opportunities for him to learn. They trusted

Figure 7–4
Zachary: Four o'clock " 'pointment."

him to create appropriate strategies to meet the challenges he set for himself.

From Family Learning to Formal Instructional Invitations

Classroom teachers can use the same decision-making process as Zachary's parents did. It is important that they consider their observations in light of what they know about learning and then make curricular decisions. The decision-making cycle that has been most useful in Tim's transition first-grade classroom follows this process. Although it is modeled after Clyde's work in a classroom setting (1986), it also represents what parents do quite naturally. This model capitalizes on the importance of using the child as curricular informant.

The way for teachers to develop such a curriculum is to record events that occur in their classrooms and then reflect on the significance of these events. Through the construction and interpretation of these classroom stories, supportive curriculum planning can emerge. Wells asserts, "Stories are one of the most effective ways of making one's own interpretation of events and ideas available to others" (1986, p. 194). Just as Zachary's mother found storytelling a useful way to reflect upon and share her understanding of her child's thinking, stories about actual classroom experiences enable teachers to understand better the children and the curriculum. The stories serve a much greater purpose than simply recollecting the day's events. They are a part of the cyclical process that guides curricular decision making. The stories emerge from classroom observations, which are analyzed for underlying meanings and theoretical significance. Teachers can then make curricular decisions and plan the next steps, as the cycle of observation begins again. This curricular decision-making cycle may be conceptualized as shown in Figure 7–5.

Decision Making in the Transition First-Grade Classroom

We continually observe children, reflect upon and interpret those observations, and make plans for future classroom experiences.

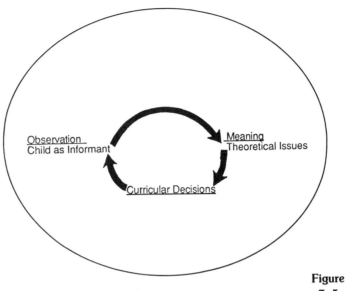

**Figure
7–5
Curricular decision-making cycle**

These new experiences then provide further opportunities for observation, interpretation, and curricular decisions.

We have found a three-column planning sheet most helpful to document the teaching-learning cycle in our room. The following represents one day's observations:

Observation	*Meaning*	*Plans*
Helpful to have various experiences planned in the morning (David—egg graph; Heidi—book order graph; Tim—egg prediction, brine shrimp).	Although kids could choose to engage or not, these experiences demonstrated functional uses of reading, writing, and mathematics.	Continue to provide such options.

Kids are beginning to use the language of adults in the room, in their discussions about writing and mathematics.
Ex: "I have a good idea . . ."
    "I noticed that . . ."
    "I found out . . ."
	Language can direct thought as well as reflect thought. Strategy-sharing sessions may have provided the children with these language demonstrations.	Continue to provide language that promotes reflection and observation.

Observation	Meaning	Plans
Kids' ideas were brilliant for their first letters to pen pals. They asked thoughtful questions and had good ideas to share with others.	They called on past reading and writing experiences to make sense of this new experience. We should not underestimate their potential for making sense out of new experiences.	Tim thinks it is important to demonstrate reading and writing processes and to examine the strategies children are using.
The song books about Tools the baby rabbit have been great. Kids love to "sing" the text.	Important to use materials they value. They extended the meaning of the songs in their own way through their illustrations.	Send Tools books home and ask parents to respond to the books by writing positive comments about their reading, writing, and art.
Games kids made: · all had dangers · some had dice · some had chips · Curtis put 2 and 6 on a chip · Tray used a spinner · Curtis painted his game	Open-ended nature of experience provided kids the opportunity to demonstrate their knowledge of games.	Share with group to highlight their strategies.
In creating the class phonebook the kids wanted to fill every line. Not a bit hesitant, very conscientious. Aaron had interesting map with school house and landmarks. Kids using the books to call others at home.	Lines on paper somewhat controlling yet helped to organize texts. Functional use of numbers and addresses was highlighted.	Talk about dash between numbers so children will understand its purpose. Encourage other map-making ventures, particularly in the block area.
Kids fascinated with clocks after the introduction about clocks that show different transition times during the school day. Kids asked interesting questions about how clocks work and the connections between the class clock and others.	Mathematics provides a system for measuring.	Make paper watches. Use timer more. Bring in an old clock to take apart to examine how it works.
Kids are not reading their own books during quiet reading time.	They do not seem to value their own publications as much as professional authors.	Read class books more during gathering. Also display the children's books in a more inviting way.

This form is effective for us because it is brief, yet thorough; it grounds instructional decisions in observations of children; and it causes us to reflect upon our curricular decisions and to question our theoretical beliefs.

The patterns from our daily observations of children in this transition first-grade classroom fall into three basic categories that represent features of a comprehensive curriculum: the curriculum as a vehicle for empowerment, the curriculum as a web of potentialities, and the curriculum as a process of meaningful communication. We will address these categories in the following pages, including examples from various classrooms (preschool through sixth grade) to demonstrate the potential of a learning-centered curriculum. Teachers may work under diverse conditions, but when they view their children and themselves as curricular decision makers they come to be more reflective about their teaching and more appreciative of children's literacy responses.

What Is Curriculum?

In this book we have described the mathematical experiences that this group of twenty six-year-olds encountered during their year in a transition first-grade classroom. They were children who were recognized by the school authorities as having "multiple deficits," yet they showed themselves to be competent and inventive problem solvers and decision makers when given the support to learn through meaningful experiences.

However, how does one effectively develop a responsive mathematics curriculum that meets the needs and interests of all students? Let us begin by sharing three definitions of curriculum and outlining their implications for an effective mathematics program. Our three definitions are not meant to be mutually exclusive, but to highlight certain aspects of a functional mathematics curriculum.

CURRICULUM AS A VEHICLE FOR EMPOWERMENT

"Curriculum is a purposeful intent to empower learners" (Burke and Short 1988). By empowering learners, we mean that they become increasingly aware of the rich complexity of mathematical uses. They come to understand the purposes, processes, and content that can be expressed through the mathematical system. Curriculum then becomes the exploration and expansion of the communication potential of this system (Harste, Woodward, and Burke 1984). Children need multiple opportunities to explore the many purposes of mathematics—measuring dinosaurs, collecting preferences, tabulating the daily attendance, dividing some freshly baked cookies, recording the daily weather conditions, or figuring the cost of a class field trip. Children gain further insights when they encounter a variety of mathematical problems and must decide upon the appropriate procedural option—estimation, mental calculation, a calculator, or pencil and paper. Each has its appropriate use. Sometimes it is more efficient to estimate: Do I have more than $30 worth of groceries in my cart? At other times mental computation is more convenient: How much is $197 + $28? (Think: $(197 + 3) + (28 - 3) = 200 + 25 = 225$.) Even though some educators have decried the use of calculators in school, these machines do have appropriate uses: How many milk cartons are consumed by our school in one year? Sometimes paper and pencil are the most efficient tools for solving problems, such as tallying votes to decide what color to paint the class puppet theater.

Children need time to explore the processes of the mathematics system itself; they must be encouraged to record their mathematical observations in their own way. They must have time to pursue interesting patterns and numerical relationships that they notice. This is not to say that children should avoid learning the basic facts. On the contrary, they need to commit these facts to memory so they can use them accurately and efficiently. However, learning these facts will be easier and more meaningful if children have opportunities to explore the various counting patterns and numerical relationships that exist between these facts. Mathematics is a system of relationships, not of isolated facts and figures.

The rush to learn basic facts by rote has plagued mathematics instruction for years. In his study entitled *A Place Called School* (1984), John Goodlad expressed this same concern:

The impression I get from topics, materials, and tests of the curriculum is of mathematics as a body of fixed facts and skills to be acquired, not as a tool for developing a particular kind of intellectual power in the study. One might expect to see by the upper elementary years activities designed to use basic skills previously acquired; instead, these skills reappear as ends in themselves. Interestingly, mathematics teachers somewhat more than teachers in the other academic subjects perceived themselves as seeking in their students processes related more to learning how to learn than to merely acquiring mechanics. Many wanted their students to be logical thinkers, to learn how to attack problems, and to think for themselves. Why, then, did so few mathematics teachers in our sample appear to get much beyond a relatively rote kind of teaching and textbook dependency not likely to develop powers of critical reasoning? (pp. 209–10)

Children are tested on the bits and pieces of mathematics. The understanding of concepts is often ignored to the exclusion of the more immediate facts and algorithms. This "Betty Crocker" approach to mathematics instruction has its natural consequences. Many children entering middle school are ill prepared for algebra because their understanding of mathematical relationships has been largely ignored. Many middle-school teachers will readily admit that students come to them with little understanding of such concepts as place value or equivalence. If educators are not careful even the area of problem solving may fall prey to this trivial pursuit theory of mathematical learning. The marketplace is inundated with books and programs that lay out problem-solving skills in a recipelike manner: present this skill, discuss that example, and assign these problems. Such programs easily lead to the same rote, isolated, worksheet-dominated experience to which students have already been subjected.

Watson and Crowley (1988) view this type of mathematical instruction as a paint-by-number theory of learning. When one paints by number, there is no attempt to integrate one part of the painting with another. Instead, 3s are blindly colored in red and 6s are dutifully colored in green, but the relationship between colors is never addressed. By contrast, when true artists create paintings, they use what they know about the mixtures of colors and the moods of certain color schemes to design an overall effect. So too should it be with mathematics instruction. Children must do more than "color in" computational facts and "shade in" specific skills; instead, they need opportunities to create by using mathematics through whole, meaning-centered experiences.

Rote learning also places an undue emphasis on convention. Although some teachers have encouraged children to develop their own ways of recording mathematical observations and their own variations of the standard algorithm (Madell 1985, Hamic 1986), most instruction still views convention as the primary goal. It focuses on the narrow goals of teaching children the standard way of constructing graphs, writing equations, or following the proper algorithmic procedures. Such instruction falsely assumes that if children are simply able to write numerical relationships conventionally, they understand these relationships. However, understanding of numerical signs and symbols comes from active engagement in the process. Children will come to appreciate the standard method of calculation when they are given the opportunity to work it out in their own way first. As children formulate knowledge for themselves, they gain insight into the principles upon which the standard algorithm is based. If the external trappings of convention become the focal point of instruction, then there is little value placed on learners' attempts to construct those meanings for themselves.

An appropriate antonym for empowerment is vulnerability. If children are ignorant of the various contexts of mathematical use, then they become vulnerable to its misuses. Children become less vulnerable when they are encouraged to do two things: First, they should ask questions about numerical information. When children spend countless hours in school merely "number crunching" and are not exposed to the various purposes for which people use numbers, they often come to believe that there is an inherent truth in anything numerical. Essays, books, plays, paintings, and such all distort the truth, they think, but numbers do not lie. Children need to develop a healthy skepticism toward numerical information. In the transition classroom the children often challenged the results of graphs. This kind of healthy vigilance over numerical information makes children more informed consumers and citizens, as well as more critical thinkers.

Second, children also become less vulnerable to the misuses of the mathematical system if they are encouraged to ask "Why?" If children are taught to memorize a series of steps to solve a problem or complete an algorithm, then the only support they can fall back on is a series of procedures that the teacher has transmitted to them. As a result, children often confuse the steps of one algorithm for another because these sequences of rules are their only guides. Vygotsky's warning must be heeded: "When the manipulation of symbols becomes paramount, to the exclusion of understanding, then the child has not mastered the system of mathematics but, on the contrary, has become imprisoned by it" (Donaldson 1978, p. 102). However, if children are challenged to create their own procedures as well as explain why some of the traditional algorithms work as they do, they gain a deeper understanding of the process and can rely on insight, rather than memory, to solve other problems that they may encounter. Richard Hemming's well-known motto, "The purpose of computing is insight, not number" (Davis and Hersh 1986), fits the intent of this discussion. One of the leading mathematics educators who focuses on the importance of asking "why" is Marilyn Burns. Her writings and videotape series highlight the value of focusing on the processes of the mathematical system (1986, 1988).

Tammy's experience underscores the importance of asking why (Whitin 1989a). This third grader had learned in an informal way about the compensation principle in her work with addition. She discovered that she could add a certain value to one addend and subtract that same value from another addend and the sum would remain the same. For instance, $6 + 7$ was the same as $(6 - 1) + (7 + 1)$, or $5 + 8$. Thus, she saw that $6 + 7$ and $5 + 8$ both equaled 13 and she could use blocks to prove it. She would often use this trick as she added. As she began her work with multiplication, Tammy wondered whether this law of compensation could be applied to this operation as well.

"Does 6×7 equal 5×8?" she asked.

"Try to find a way to figure it out," her teacher responded.

Soon she presented the results. "It doesn't work. 6×7 is 42 and 5×8 is only 40. It worked when you added numbers. Why doesn't it work now?"

This "why" question was the impetus for an interesting mathematical investigation. Tammy used some graph paper and drew some arrays to try to discover the answer to her question. However, the important point to be made here is that this "why" question encouraged Tammy to explore and expand her knowledge of the mathematics system. She gained a broader understanding of the operations of addition and multiplication and an insight into the compensation law of mathematics. Asking "why" pushes learners beyond the right answer and forces them to focus on the process. It also fosters a spirit of mutual inquisitiveness in the classroom. When children sense that their queries are respected, they are more willing to verbalize hunches, make predictions, and take further risks in exploring numerical patterns and relationships. In this kind of classroom one cannot always predict the kind of questions that will be asked or the kind of investigations that will be carried out. Children are constructors, not passive recipients, of their mathematical knowledge, and their questions reflect their current perceptions and understanding of this communication system.

CURRICULUM AS A WEB OF POTENTIALITIES OR POSSIBILITIES

When children have a voice in curriculum planning it is difficult to predict all that will happen in a given school year. Good curriculum planning involves capitalizing on the interests and experiences of the children themselves. From this perspective there is no such phenomenon as disadvantaged children. Their experiences and knowledge of the world are viewed as assets for learning. In the transition classroom the children knew a lot about teeth. They all had teeth stories to tell because these stories were tied to an experience that they knew something about. However, this view of curriculum has not always been reflected in the mathematical organization and content of many schools.

Too often mathematics is unconnected to the lives of children. When children spend countless hours doing only computational exercises they lose sight of the varied and purposeful role of mathematics. However, sometimes students quietly rebel. One third-grade boy admitted that when he is faced with a long page of computations, "I just make up some story problems so I know what the numbers mean." A fifth-grade student, who used to dislike math but now enjoys it, explained his sudden change of attitude in this way: "I just pretended the numbers were money—all money. I love money!" These anecdotes illustrate that mathematics had become so decontextualized, so removed from the lives of students, that learners had to create their own context to restore meaning. "A word without meaning is an empty sound" (Vygotsky 1962, p. 120). So too with numbers. For these children mathematics had become a hollow experience. In their own way they sought to resurrect and preserve the wholeness of the mathematics language.

One way to connect mathematics to the lives of children is to capitalize on their interests. April's drawing of the mother fish with her seven babies, which she posted above the fish tank, led Tim to invite other children to tell fish stories. Tim's curricular decisions were not just made for the children, but with the children. Another example of following a child's lead occurred in a third-grade classroom. Children were spending a lot of time jumping rope on the playground. The teacher noticed this keen interest and ability and encouraged them to record their chants for others to hear. A tape was made, as well as a class book. Several of the rhymes contained the counting-on patterns of twos, fives, and tens. The children colored these numerical patterns on a hundred-square sheet and noted relationships that they saw. In the transition classroom the children also showed a fascination for jumping rope. Every day as they came in from recess they shared their own personal record for the number of consecutive jumps. They praised each other's accomplishments and even applauded for a beginner named Curtis when he successfully made two jumps. Their interest in personal jumping records encouraged Tim to give them some graph paper to record their daily totals.

Another example occurred in a third-grade classroom when the children demonstrated a strong interest in shooting marbles. As the teacher watched the children more closely on the playground he noticed that some marbles were worth more than others. Indeed, the children had devised their own language and exchange rate for the various marbles they were using: littlies, cat's eyes, purees, biggies, biggie-jumbos, jumbos, and steelies (ball bearings) all had a value of increasing worth. The teacher invited the children to explain their system of exchange with the rest of the class and to pose exchanging problems for each other: "If I gave you a jumbo, how many purees would you have to give me for it?" Their marbles proved to be an excellent nonproportional model for a place-value system. All these examples show how the web of curricular possibilities can be developed if teachers capitalize on what the children already know.

Another strategy for incorporating the voice of children into curricular planning is to seize the moment. In a third-grade classroom a teacher was intending to work with a group of children about odd and even numbers. A large pile of one-inch cubes lay on the table, and the teacher gave the children some time to build their own patterns and designs before he began his own planned investigation. At one point several of the children began to make successively larger squares: $2 \times 2, 3 \times 3, 4 \times 4$, and so on. One child looked at his 3×3 square and remarked, "Hey, look, there's a 2×2 square hidden inside it!" He slid out the 2×2 pattern to show the group his discovery. The teacher sensed the interest in this discovery and seized the opportunity to extend the investigation: "How many 2×2 squares can you find in other squares? Is there a pattern to your results?" The children spent several days at home and at school uncovering some intriguing patterns because the teacher capitalized on the moment to extend their initial discovery (Whitin 1979).

The curriculum can also become a web of possibilities when children are engaged in open-ended experiences. These kinds of experiences require no pre- or postcriterion levels for entry or exit. Instead, all children can participate; they can construct their own meanings and ask their own questions. Reading a children's literature book that has a mathematical focus to it and then inviting the children to respond to that story through drama, writing, or illustrations is one example of an open-ended invitation. Another example occurred in a fourth-grade classroom when the teacher presented the class with a money alphabet: $a = 1¢, b = 2¢, c = 3¢ \ldots z = 26¢$. He challenged the children to find out how much their name was worth and anything else they could discover. Children began comparing their names with their peers and some investigated the name values for other family members. Some children sought to find the cheapest and most expensive states in the United States. Others who enjoyed baseball tried to find the most expensive team. There was a group who set more general challenges: What is the cheapest three-letter word? The most expensive one? Are there any words worth exactly one dollar? Some reached to find dictionaries while others thumbed through magazines and encyclopedias. They set their own challenges because the open-ended nature of the experience encouraged their multiple responses.

CURRICULUM AS A PROCESS OF MEANINGFUL COMMUNICATION

Douglas Barnes (1987) sees curriculum as a process of continual discourse. There is time in classrooms to converse about different solutions to a given problem. There is time to read books and discuss what role mathematics plays in telling the stories. There is time to collaborate with peers and teachers in solving mathematical problems. There is time to defend as well as challenge certain conclusions drawn from numerical data. It is this exchange of ideas, solutions, and interpretations that infuses the classroom atmosphere with a vibrance for discovery and investigation. Unfortunately, many mathematical classrooms are too silent. Children can usually be found bent over desks completing worksheets or task cards in silence. Part of the blame lies with a misconstrued notion of individualized instruction. The zealous desire to meet individual needs has preempted the social aspect of learning. It is a sad irony that children attend this social institution called school, surrounded by hundreds of peers, and yet spend most of their time in isolation. Some teachers see little need for talking. There are certain procedures to know, and children need time to practice them. One cannot talk about numbers in the same way one can discuss *Treasure Island* or the history of Egypt. However, this argument fails to consider that mathematics is a language too. Mathematics is a way of describing what we observe in the world and a means of sharing that information with others. Speech is another communication system through which learners can express ideas and reflect on their own thinking. Jerome Bruner (1968) has long advocated the critical role that language plays in cognitive development, but his recommendation seems to have gone unheeded in many mathematics classrooms. Students are largely controlled by the worksheet, which insulates them from each other and keeps control firmly in the hands of the teacher (Barnes 1987). However, language can be a powerful vehicle for enabling children to express what they know and how they know it; as children use language to frame their experiences, the very act of reflection can often generate new knowledge (Harste, Woodward, and Burke 1984). Oral language plays a critical role in promoting mathematical understanding.

Effective classroom teachers perceive curriculum as a meaning exchange. Time is provided for children to pose questions

("How can I change this recipe so I make enough cookies for the class?"), to make observations ("Hey, I notice something very strange. Vanilla and chocolate each have five votes"), to venture predictions ("The longest dinosaur would probably reach all the way to the tennis courts"), and to wonder ("How many blades of grass are there on this playground?"). This kind of communication is possible in a classroom that values children's questions, ideas, and observations.

Joining the Literacy Club in Mathematics

Frank Smith (1988) argues that children become proficient readers and writers only when they are admitted to a community of language users, which he has called the "literacy club." Children are admitted before they can even read or write a single word and are supported by more experienced members as they engage in functional and meaningful endeavors. This same perspective can be applied to the development of mathematical literacy. Children learn to use mathematics efficiently when they become members of a mathematics club—a community of users who view mathematics as a tool for learning. Children are admitted to this club even before they can write a number or understand an equals sign. Members give each other support as they become involved in enterprises that demonstrate the value and utility of mathematics to new members. Members do not learn an abstract system of mathematics first and then attempt to apply it to various contexts; instead, they learn about mathematics as they use it.

As teachers seek learning experiences that promote the functional use of the mathematics system, it is important that they develop some general strategies for fostering its growth. Some of these include the following.

First, *involve children in the decision-making processes of the school.* What specific problems have arisen in the school? How can children gather data to help document the problem as well as offer possible solutions? In one school students were irritated by the long wait in the cafeteria lunch lines. They developed surveys on who was dissatisfied and analyzed the length of time different classes had to wait. The results were reported to the cafeteria personnel, who worked with the students to propose possible solutions. At another school a pre-school program was allotted some additional funds to buy some more playground vehicles. The teacher allowed the children to decide how those funds ought to be spent. She conducted a class meeting so the children could discuss the advantages and disadvantages of purchasing each vehicle: big wheels, trikes, wagons, and so on. Then they constructed a graph to determine the preferences of the group. At another school an architect-in-residence was hired for a short period of time to assist the children in redesigning their playground. A selected group of students worked with the architect on this project. They sub-mitted drawings of how to use the playground space more efficiently. Some were involved in creating scale drawings and models of the area; others conducted surveys and gathered information about the most popular piece of playground equip-ment. Their enthusiasm and dedication for this project were unflagging because they knew their efforts would be respected; the decisions they were making would help to satisfy a genuine need. At still another school the library received some special funding to buy new books. Children devised surveys to as-certain the kind of books that students most wanted in the library. They compiled their results into a graph and presented their findings to the librarian.

On another occasion some sixth-grade students assisted the principal in determining the size and placement of various bul-letin boards throughout the school. They took measurements of several locations and used paper models to ascertain the number of 4×8 sheets of homosote needed to complete the project (Whitin 1987). Principals can play a key role in involving children in a wide variety of decisions that concern building maintenance, improvement, and design. In a third-grade class-room the children played an active role in designing their own learning environment. This teacher felt strongly that the chil-dren should not enter a classroom at the beginning of the year that was fully equipped. Instead, one of the tasks that the children were involved in during their first day at school was to unpack boxes of supplies that had been ordered during the summer. The children were responsible for establishing their own classification scheme for the books in the class library. The price tags were purposely left on all materials so that the children were reminded of the financial resources needed to fund their classroom. In other classrooms children have been involved in designing curtains for their windows, building benches to sit on during their class meetings, and constructing a loft so they would have a quiet place to read. Some have even fashioned stilts, one of their favorite pieces of playground equipment. Children come to appreciate and respect their classroom environment when they take an active role in creating parts of it themselves.

All these examples demonstrate the learning opportunities for children who are invited to participate in the decision-making process of their school.

Second, *design ways to incorporate mathematics into the daily life of the classroom.* For instance, there are many opportunities for graphing. In one classroom children read the thermometer every morning and recorded their findings on a large sheet of graph paper. This task was completed at the same time every day during their morning meeting. As the year progressed the children had the opportunity to view the general temperature trends of their area. On another occasion a teacher used a graph as a vehicle to determine which book he was going to read aloud that day. Children perused the three books that were on display and chose the one they wanted to hear.

Other teachers have incorporated mathematical ideas as part of their daily routine during the morning meeting. Children sign their names on a chart every morning, and the children interpret that chart as they discuss the day's attendance. Some teachers will extend this discussion by asking, "How many noses are here today? How many eyes? thumbs? fingers? elbows? ears? freckles?" Such questions provide a fruitful introduction to repeated addition as well as an interesting discussion about estimation. One teacher posed a slightly different question by asking, "How many pockets are here today?" (Burns 1988). At one point the children put a cube in each pocket and then snapped them together in sets of ten to find the total. They kept track of the number of pockets for one week and then graphed the results.

Some teachers have a monthly calendar and encourage the children to make observations about what they see: "We don't go to school on the 20th"; "There are four Fridays in this month"; or "The Thursdays change from odd (5) to even (12) to odd (19) to even (26)." Other teachers keep track of items that the class is collecting (egg cartons for a science project, bottle caps for an art project, or soup labels for a fund-raising effort) and share that information at the morning meeting. The daily total is always discussed. "John brought in eight bottle caps and Sarah brought in seven. How would you find the total for today?" asks the teacher. Children share their thinking strategies, such as doubling seven and adding one more, or doubling eight and subtracting one. It is an opportune time to share mathematical thinking in the context of a meaningful task. Another teacher set up a bulletin board entitled "Numbers in the News" and encouraged children to find articles in newspapers and magazines that use numbers. The functions of these numbers were discussed in class. Another teacher who was reading a chapter-length book would write the page number on the board every day. As he wrote page 55 one day some of the children were intrigued by that pattern.

"Hey, that has two 5s, 55," one child remarked.

"Yes, that's like 66 and 77," replied another. Soon the pattern of 11, 22, 33, and so on was recorded on the board and then colored in on a hundred-square sheet so it could be seen in a different way. This discovery was made possible by a teacher who kept demonstrating the functional use of numbers in his classroom. In this way mathematics became a natural part of the life of a classroom.

Third, *capitalize on field trips and other special school events.* Every fall a third- and fourth-grade class climbed a mountain. Afterwards the children documented the event in various ways: they wrote stories, created paintings, devised captions for the photographs taken, and constructed numerous surveys. Some of the questions they wanted to have answered were: What did you bring to eat and drink? Who brought a canteen? What did you wear on your feet? How many times did you stop to rest? How many layers did you wear? Their findings, along with their stories, paintings, and photographs, were brought together in a mural that nicely documented the total experience. On another occasion a fourth-grade class was organizing a field day for the kindergarten. In order to ensure that the event would be successful the older students conducted numerous surveys to obtain information that they thought was essential: What kinds of races do you like best? Do you like events when you work with a partner? When you get hot, what is your favorite thing to drink? On another occasion a fifth-grade classroom was planning a trip to a museum. The teacher encouraged the children to figure out all the details for this upcoming excursion. Some students wrote letters to the museum to ascertain admission fees. Others called the bus company to obtain the cost per mile for using the bus and the hourly rate for the driver. Other students determined the number of chaperones needed. The class felt strongly that the admission fee for the chaperones ought to be absorbed by the total class; thus, the cost per student had to be recalculated to accommodate this concern. These classroom examples stress the importance of using special school events to extend mathematical learning.

Fourth, *look for ways to integrate mathematics into other subject areas*. In a first-grade classroom children were growing mung beans in a long window box to feed their rabbit. They kept track of the growth of their plants by constructing a graph using paper strips. In a sixth-grade science class some students were using graphs to show the longevity of various brands of batteries. In a third-grade social studies class children were conducting surveys to determine how far away from home people had traveled. On another occasion a fourth-grade class studying nutrition was gathering information on the eating habits of their schoolmates. A first-grade class was using rulers to mark off the lengths of various dinosaurs on the wall in their corridor. In a third-grade classroom the children were creating books entitled "All About Me." On one occasion the teacher challenged them by posing this problem: "Find out as much as you can about yourself by using this measuring tape." The children recorded a variety of body measurements in their notebooks. During a unit on winter survival some fourth-grade students used some pine strapping from a local lumberyard to build their own set of snowshoes. These classroom examples testify to the omnipresence of mathematics in all areas and demonstrate the usefulness of mathematics as a language to document change and convey ideas.

Summary

Mathematical literacy will never be found in a workbook, skill sheet, or basal mathematics text. No publisher will ever be able to package it, contain it, or sell it. True mathematical literacy must originate not from a methodology but from a theory of learning—one that views mathematics not as a series of formulas, calculations, or even problem-solving techniques, but as a way of knowing and learning about the world. Teachers facilitate this learning in the following ways.

1. *By capitalizing on the interests of their students.* The children in the transition first-grade classroom had a compelling interest in dinosaurs and were given the opportunity to explore and expand that interest. They shared what they already knew about dinosaurs, posed questions they wanted to have answered, identified resources they could consult, and devised ways to share their knowledge with others. They used mathematics as a tool to investigate both the size and weight of dinosaurs and their time in history, and to tell their own personal dinosaur stories. What are your children's interests, and how might you capitalize on these to build a curriculum responsive to their needs?

2. *By extending what children already know.* The children in the transition first-grade classroom knew about losing and growing teeth. They used mathematics to demonstrate that knowledge. What are your children's areas of expertise, and how can you connect the lives of these students with the curriculum of your classroom?

3. *By building on classroom events.* Even though it was unsuccessful, the classroom fish tank proved to be a learning experience, because the children used mathematics to create their own tales about fish. What events have occurred in your classroom that you could build on to extend learning?

4. *By providing a time for strategy sharing.* Our children shared potential meanings for zero as well as insights about the mathematical system through the use of their fingers. A diversity of responses and solution strategies was encouraged. The children soon became familiar with one of our favorite axioms: "It's far better to solve one problem three different ways than three problems the same way." Jermaine cogently summarized the value of these sharing sessions when he responded to one child's thinking strategy, "Hey, I never even thought of that!" When in your schedule can you provide time for children to share their mathematical insights?

5. *By encouraging children to invent their own system of recording mathematical ideas.* Even though their equations and graphs can sometimes look like random marks from

an adult perspective, children's explanations of these marks reflect a way of knowing that is systematic, organized, and meaningful. Children need opportunities to view standard methods for constructing graphs and performing calculations as well as the freedom to explore these tools themselves to solve their own problems and convey their own ideas. How can you provide opportunities for children to share their understanding of mathematical concepts by creating their own methods of recording?

6. *By incorporating children's literature into the mathematics program.* Books provide a meaningful context for number use; mathematics becomes embedded in an authentic experience from which children can construct their own interpretations. The children in the transition first-grade classroom recited "Five Little Monkeys" during their animal study and read *Seven Eggs* during their dinosaur enterprise. Their responses demonstrated unique understandings about the addition and subtraction processes. How can you incorporate mathematical stories into your own themes of study?

7. *By setting up literate environments that emphasize the functionality of number use.* Mathematics is everywhere. There is a plethora of measuring devices—scales of all kinds, tapes, rulers, measuring spoons, cups, even a device for measuring your shoe size donated by the local shoe store. There are surveys, calendars, phonebooks, clocks, grocery receipts, newspapers, magazines, blueprints, recipes, and collections of all kinds. There are photographs of the school and the neighborhood that document number use: on automobiles, bridges, road signs, stores, offices, and so on. What materials can you gather together to demonstrate the functional use of numbers in various contexts?

A Final Story

The children in this transition first-grade classroom had been studying animals for nearly two months. They had shared knowledge of animals with each other and then posed questions they wanted to have answered. They brought to school a wide variety of books, magazines, and articles; the children shared these resources with each other while Tim read others aloud to the group; predictable books about animals were read together as a class and then taped for others to listen to independently. The children wrote animal stories and created puppet shows, paintings, sculptures, and illustrations to show what they were learning. There was a constant hum of discussion, questioning, and debate about aspects of animal life that the children wondered about—their diet, defense, size, and strength.

As a culminating experience for this animal study the children went on a field trip to the nearby city zoo. Part of their time was spent with a docent who showed the children various birds, snakes, and other animals. He asked these six-year-olds a series of questions about reptiles and mammals. The children not only responded eagerly to his questions but asked him some intriguing ones of their own. Obviously impressed by the depth of their knowledge and the insight of their questions, the docent turned to Tim and asked, "Excuse me, but is this a gifted and talented class?"

How does a book that began with a group of children who were deemed not ready for first grade and who had "multiple deficits" conclude with the same group of children who are now perceived as gifted and talented? What has changed? They are the same children, but their classroom environment has changed to provide them increased opportunities to demonstrate what they know. As Elliot Eisner so aptly remarked, "Lack of talent is oftentimes nothing more than an excuse for absence of opportunity" (1981). In this room there was no lack of talent. Indeed, talent abounded because there were ample opportunities for children to use multiple communication systems, including mathematics, as vehicles for recording observations and exploring questions that they were interested in pursuing. Good curriculum development demonstrates ever-increasing options for learners. Only in this manner will our understanding of mathematical literacy be broadened, as teachers and children live and learn mathematics together.

REFERENCES

Anno, Mitsumasa. 1977. *Anno's Counting Book*. New York: Thomas Crowell.

Barnes, Douglas. 1987. *From Communication to Curriculum*. New York: Penguin Books.

Baum, L. Frank. 1904. *The Land of Oz*. Chicago: Reilly and Lee.

Biggs, Edith, and Robert McClean. 1969. *Freedom to Learn*. Reading, Mass.: Addison-Wesley.

Bridwell, Norman. 1966. *Clifford's Halloween*. New York: Scholastic.

Bright, Robert. 1944. *Georgie*. New York: Scholastic.

Brown, Stephen. 1974. "Musing on Multiplication." *Mathematics Teaching* 61: 26–30.

Brown, Stephen, and Marion Walter. 1983. *The Art of Problem Posing*. Hillsdale, N.J.: Lawrence Erlbaum Associates.

Bruner, Jerome. 1968. *Toward a Theory of Instruction*. New York: W. W. Norton.

Burke, Carolyn, and Kathy Short. 1988. "Creating Curriculums Which Foster Thinking." In *Critical Thinking*, ed. by Jerome Harste. Urbana, Ill.: National Council of Teachers of English.

Burns, Marilyn. 1986. "Teaching 'What to Do' in Arithmetic vs. Teaching 'What To Do and Why.'" *Educational Leadership* (April): 34–38.

————. 1988. *Mathematics with Manipulatives*. Videotape series. New Rochelle, N.Y.: Cuisenaire Company.

Clyde, Jean Anne. 1986. *Creating Literate Environments for Preschool Children: Teachers as Participants, Demonstrators, Researchers, and Learners*. Ph.D. diss., Indiana University, Bloomington, In.

Davis, Philip, and Reuben Hersh. 1981. *The Mathematical Experience*. Boston: Houghton Mifflin.

————. 1986. *The World According to Descartes*. Boston: Houghton Mifflin.

Donaldson, Margaret. 1978. *Children's Minds*. New York: W. W. Norton and Co.

Dr. Seuss. 1938. *The 500 Hats of Bartholomew Cubbins*. New

York: Vanguard Publishing Co.

——. 1960. *One Fish, Two Fish, Red Fish, Blue Fish.* New York: Random House.

——. 1963. *Hop on Pop.* New York: Random House.

Einstein, Albert. 1945. Letter. In *The Psychology of Invention in the Mathematical Field,* ed. by Jacques Hadamard. Princeton, N.J.: Princeton University Press.

Eisner, Elliot. 1981. "The Role of the Arts in Cognition and Curriculum." *Phi Delta Kappa* 63: 48–55.

Gardner, Howard. 1983. *Frames of Mind.* New York: Basic Books.

Goodlad, John. 1984. *A Place Called School.* New York: McGraw-Hill.

Goss, Janet, and Jerome Harste. 1981. *It Didn't Frighten Me.* New York: School Fair Books.

Halliday, M. A. K. 1975. *Learning How to Mean: Explorations in the Development of Language.* London: Edward Arnold.

——. 1978. *Language as a Social Semiotic: The Social Interpretation of Language and Meaning.* Baltimore, Md.: University Park Press.

Hamic, Eleanor. 1986. "Students' Creative Computations: My Way or Your Way." *Arithmetic Teacher* 34 (September): 39–41.

Harste, Jerome C., and Kathy G. Short, with Carolyn Burke. 1988. *Creating Classrooms for Authors: The Reading–Writing Connection.* Portsmouth, N.H.: Heinemann.

Harste, Jerome C.; Virginia A. Woodward; and Carolyn L. Burke. 1984. *Language Stories & Literacy Lessons.* Portsmouth, N.H.: Heinemann.

Hoff, Syd. 1958. *Danny and the Dinosaur.* New York: Harper and Row.

Hooper, Meredith. 1985. *Seven Eggs.* New York: Harper and Row.

John-Steiner, Vera. 1985. *Notebooks of the Mind: Explorations of Thinking.* Albuquerque, N.M.: University of New Mexico.

Krauss, Ruth. 1945. *The Carrot Seed.* New York: Harper and Row.

Kuhn, Thomas. 1970. *The Structure of Scientific Revolutions.* Chicago: University of Chicago Press.

Madell, Rob. 1985. "Children's Natural Processes." *Arithmetic Teacher* 33 (March): 20–22.

National Council of Teachers of Mathematics. 1980. *An Agenda for Action: Recommendations for School Mathematics of the 1980s*. Reston, Va.: National Council of Teachers of Mathematics.

———. 1989. *Curriculum and Evaluation Standards for School Mathematics*. Reston, Va.: National Council of Teachers of Mathematics.

O'Keefe, Timothy. In press. "A Day with Dinosaurs." In *Portraits of Whole Language Classrooms*, ed. by Heidi Mills and Jean Anne Clyde. Portsmouth, N.H.: Heinemann.

Reys, Barbara. 1986. "Estimation and Mental Computation: It's 'About' Time." *Arithmetic Teacher* 34 (September): 22–23.

Rowe, D. W. 1986. *Literacy in the Child's World: Preschoolers' Explorations of Alternate Sign Systems*. Ph.D. diss., Indiana University, Bloomington, In.

Sacks, Oliver. 1985. *The Man Who Mistook His Wife for a Hat and Other Clinical Tales*. New York: Simon & Schuster.

Smith, Frank. 1988. *Joining the Literacy Club: Further Essays into Education*. Portsmouth, N.H.: Heinemann.

Sullivan, Joan. 1972. "Round as a Pancake." In *Sounds of Home*, ed. by Bill Martin. New York: Holt, Rinehart.

Watson, Dorothy; Carolyn Burke; and Jerome Harste. 1989. *Whole Language: Inquiring Voices*. New York: Scholastic.

Watson, Dorothy, and Paul Crowley. 1988. "How Can We Implement a Whole-Language Approach?" In *Reading Process and Practice: From Socio-Psycholinguistics to Whole Language*, ed. by Constance Weaver. Portsmouth, N.H.: Heinemann.

Wells, Gordon. 1986. *The Meaning Makers: Children Learning Language and Using Language to Learn*. Portsmouth, N.H.: Heinemann.

Whitin, David J. 1979. "Patterns with Square Numbers." *Arithmetic Teacher* 27 (December): 38–39.

———. 1987. "Problem Solving in Action: The Bulletin Board Dilemma." *Arithmetic Teacher* 35 (November): 48–50.

———. 1989a. "Number Sense and the Importance of Asking 'Why.'" *Arithmetic Teacher* 36 (January): 26–29.

———. 1989b. "The Power of Mathematical Investigations." *Elementary School Mathematics NCTM Yearbook*. Reston, Va.: National Council of Teachers of Mathematics.